BEING C...
TODAY

BEING CATHOLIC TODAY

FAITH, DOUBT AND EVERYDAY LIFE

Laurence McTaggart OSB

Fount
An Imprint of HarperCollins*Publishers*

Fount is an imprint of
HarperCollins*Religious*
part of HarperCollins*Publishers*
77–85 Fulham Palace Road, London W6 8JB
www.christian-publishing.com

First published in Great Britain in 2000 by Fount
This edition 2001

1 3 5 7 9 10 8 6 4 2

Scripture quotations are taken from the *Jerusalem Bible*,
© 1966 Darton, Longman and Todd Ltd and Doubleday

A catalogue record for this book
is available from the British Library

ISBN 0 00 712179 2

Printed and bound in Great Britain by
Clays Ltd, St Ives plc

for Dick and Marie-Thérèse Mardon
with thanks and love

CONTENTS

Part 4: Issues for Today

PREFACE

Do not be afraid.

Isaiah 41:14

You may think this is a book, but it's more a conversation. I'm not attempting to settle any of the problems of being a Catholic today, nor will I give any definitive account of what it means to be Catholic. Maybe those would be good things to do, but they are beyond any one person to achieve on his or her own. So, instead, I offer you one half of a conversation for you to react to as you wish. Parts you may like, and parts you may think are rubbish. Parts may even offend, in which case I ask your pardon as that was not my intention.

You may also think of things I have not talked about which matter to you very much. Treat, if you will, what follows as one Catholic trying to say what his faith is in today's world. It is part of the human condition to be confused and challenged, by faith and by the life we lead. We also yearn for sense and for vision. To find it, we have to share with each other, without too much fear. In what follows, I am trying to share what sense I have made of life so far. Indeed, the Church is made up of a lot of very different people united by one hope, of finding God and staying with him. Let us enjoy each other's company for a while, and then part, if not in agreement on everything, then at least having found a new friend with whom to talk.

Conversations often ramble, so feel free to move around and skip bits that don't appeal to you. But a key point that I want to make is that the many problems we face in the Catholic Church have to be understood not just in the context of the faith, but as *part* of the faith. The problems are what it is to be Catholic today, part of a human community that needs the redemption of God, and that tries to celebrate it in our lives as best we can. So the first few chapters are about faith and the Catholic faith, and I hope they illuminate the later ones.

Just a word of thanks to some of the people who have encouraged me with this book: my father Andrew, Fr. Bede Leach, Madeleine Judd, Andrew and Nicola Higgins, Fr. Dominic Milroy, Mark Detre, Fr. Patrick Barry, Ed Walton, Anna Reid and Fr. Roger Barralet, to name just a few. None of us stands alone before God, and I am blessed in the people I have with me, and most of all in my mother, Violet, who has gone before to encourage.

The mistakes are all mine, of course. We all make mistakes, and that is what the Church is for: a place where we can go wrong in safety and in good company, sure of forgiveness.

INTRODUCTION

Being Catholic

They have found pardon in the wilderness.

Jeremiah 21:2

A bad day

Everything seemed to be going well. The train was on time, and I had a table to myself to spread out sandwiches and books. In fact, the carriage was almost empty, and mobile phones went off less than twice a minute. So why, I wondered, did he sit next to me?

'Which parish are you from, Father?'

'I'm a monk, actually.'

Of course he turns out to be a Catholic, so what else can we talk about?

He wants to know about his children, two sons. One is something in the City, the other is on a long-haired traverse of the Antipodes. He is not sure which is more of a disappointment. They don't go to Mass, you see. He did everything God could have asked of him, and even paid for an independent Catholic education. Finally, he told them that they were in danger of losing their souls unless they submitted to the tedium of weekly Sunday Mass. He was surprised to find this did not move them. 'Now, Father,' he asked, 'are they not doomed to hell?'

I found that rather an odd question from a parent, and not at all easy to answer. He interpreted, rightly, that my silence was temporizing. I was obviously about to say that things are not that simple: typical, liberal wool-gathering. What would *you* have said that might have satisfied him? I'll tell you later what I said (see chapter

14), and you can decide if you would do any better. But for now, I would just like to log two issues for the future. First, people can say the oddest things from the best of motives. After all, the man *was* worried about his children. Second, nothing that matters in life and religion is ever simple.

Maybe both those ideas are totally obvious. But you try living by them. In practice, we ask questions in fear or doubt, and answer with anxiety or aggression. There is a thought too that religious matters should be fairly easy to understand. 'Why can't those big-oted people just read what Jesus has to say about the hypocrisy of the Pharisees?' Or, 'Why can't those people for whom anything goes just keep the rules that God has given in the Church?' The answer to both questions is that we are all *people*, and people are like that. If you are a person too, then read on, because we shall see that this is exactly the problem that God has faced in and through Jesus: how to redeem us without destroying what he has made us to be.

But first, the doomed journey continued. At Edinburgh station I escaped, and stood watching the departure board in a recuperative daydream. I had forgotten the bruising encounter, forgotten that I was in a clerical shirt, forgotten everything except that I was halfway home for a week's holiday.

Not for long – the voice was loud and insistent, 'Father, Father!' The man was standing in front of me with his face close to mine, and it dawned on me that it was me he was talking to. His name was Ian, and his general appearance such that I was not going to be anything but polite. He wanted to know about Lazarus.

'Who?' Lazarus, he explained as though to an idiot, was the man Jesus raised from the dead. Had he gone to heaven on dying or not? Because if he had, and Jesus then brought him back to earth by res-urrection, he must have been a bit ****ed off with Our Lord. I replied with honesty that I had not thought about the problem before. This he found hard to take. I was a priest, I had done all that study, and I could not answer an obvious question. 'And another thing, Father . . .' Several more questions followed, until Ian had to go and catch his train to get to Glasgow in time for his criminal trial for robbery with violence. He expected about ten years minimum. He wrung my hand and begged me to pray for him every day, espe-cially to Our Lady, who always looked after him.

In our short time together I did learn that he thought the Church was a great thing, would be lost without it, and hadn't been near a church since his marriage to a pregnant seventeen-year-old, which ended after he was sent to jail for beating her up a few months later. But he was proud to be Catholic, read his Bible and thought hard about all kinds of issues. He was also very sad about the death of Mother Teresa of Calcutta, who, he said, was his model for Christian living.

After that, I gave up, really, and was not at all surprised when a youngish man in clerical collar and neat white jacket sat next to me on the Inverness train, and struck up a conversation. We had a very pleasant talk; he was not fully informed on Lazarus either, but we agreed on many things. One exception was his vitriolic opposition to the ordination of women (I am not vitriolic). But we were one on sacraments and most of the Catholic tradition. He was a great admirer of Pope John Paul II and his strong stance on moral and doctrinal issues.

I asked him, in that case, why he did not become a Catholic. He was, you see, a member of the Anglican Communion. He replied, rather tartly, that he already was a Catholic, but that he did not feel able to become a *Roman* Catholic, and became rather tetchy. Further enquiry revealed that he felt he had a duty to look after his parishioners, who were largely of the same mind, and to 'pope' would be to abandon them. He had decided that to stay within the Anglican Church would be an effective witness to its catholic and apostolic roots.

Perhaps I should explain the problem. The Reformation in this country, starting in the sixteenth century and continuing until the late seventeenth, was not a straightforward affair, and there were always some who followed the break with Rome and papal authority, but wished to retain the Catholic doctrinal heritage: sacraments, a strong view of priesthood etc. Others wanted to adopt a fully Protestant view of the church and its life. Historically, this resulted in the compromise of a broad Anglican church, with a liturgy and structure that allowed both tendencies, 'high' and 'low', to live side by side. The more 'catholic' Anglicans tend to attach much weight to being catholic and apostolic, but still reject a strong papacy and, usually, more 'modern' doctrines, such as papal infallibility and the Immaculate Conception. At the same time, English Roman Catholics (I've run out of adjectives that satisfy everyone, but you know what I mean) tend, with justification, to be jealous of their identity as Catholic, kept through times of persecution, and say that you are either in communion with Rome or you are not Catholic.

Beats me

So, what does it mean to be *catholic*? What does it mean to be *Catholic*? Is there a difference? And why should it matter anyway? We have just met three people with different answers to all those questions. For the anguished clergyman, to be Catholic is to have beliefs that can be traced back to the apostolic church of the first century and to the words of Jesus. For the angry father, it is to belong to an organization established by Christ, and to keep the commandments it has given in his name. For the delinquent, it is to know that the Church is there, and that this means that God is with him somehow. The father would say that the vicar is catholic, perhaps, but not Catholic; the vicar would say that the father holds on to superstitions that have nothing to do with pure Catholicism; Ian, if he could articulate his thought, would say that both are stuck in irrelevant sidelines.

Jesus gives us a fairly hefty clue to our dilemma:

> Go and learn the meaning of the words: I want mercy and not sacrifice. Indeed, I have come to call the righteous, not sinners.
>
> Matthew 9:13

I'm sorry, I'll read that again:

> Go and learn the meaning of the words: I want mercy and not sacrifice. Indeed, I have come to call not the righteous, but sinners.

It is surely possible to assume that being Catholic is something to do with answering that call. My three acquaintances would each acknowledge that. Every catholic, or Catholic, is motivated by the call of Christ to follow him, or else they are not Catholic, or even catholic, at all. This does not mean that the call leads only into the Roman Catholic Church, and that people outside are not called, or do not respond fully to that call. Nor is it to say that, if the 'call' is there, it does not matter about how you act or think or what you believe, and certainly not whether you belong to any particular 'visible' church. Such questions lie ahead of us.

But Jesus' words imply a set of priorities. The context of the saying is important. He has been asked by the Pharisees why he eats with 'tax collectors and sinners'. Tax collectors were in the employ of the occupying Romans, and thus doubly unpopular as traitors to their nation and its religion. Pharisees aimed to keep the Law of Moses and the various Jewish traditions in their entirety. A sinner was, in the view of the Pharisees, anybody who was not a Pharisee. There are plenty of sinners around today, and also no lack of Pharisees. Which are you? Or are you a bit of both?

Here is a simple and relatively harmless example, but a surprisingly common one. A lady comes to confession. She doesn't have much to mention, a few cross words and the like. But she failed to go to Mass for three Sundays in a row. She knows this is so bad, she thinks it is a mortal sin. It is tempting to comfort her: 'Lots of people don't go to Mass at all for years, most people miss from time to time.' But that would be wrong because, for her, this clearly matters. So, I ask why she stayed away, and am shocked to the core by her answer. I am shocked because it reveals a far greater, more deadly fault. She missed Mass because she was confined to bed by influenza. Maybe one should laugh, tell her not to be so silly; how can you be expected to go to Mass if you are ill? After all, the sabbath was made for man, not man for the sabbath.

But that is the greater fault, and I stand indicted, along with all of you and the whole Church. This simple, obvious, common-sense message that we are only expected to attend Sunday Mass if it is physically and morally possible has been obscured. How? And why? The answer is manifold.

A 'liberal' might say that the Church has become full of legalistic misunderstandings. Following church rules is invested with a kind of magic: do this, and you will be all right. Jesus has some tough things to say about people who rely on external observances, and about those teachers who lay heavy burdens on the poor in spirit. It is only now, one might say, after the Second Vatican Council, that we are recovering the real intentions of Christ, losing the sterile additions, superstitions and clericalism of the Middle Ages and Counter-Reformation, and so coming to a true freedom. The hierarchy resists this, at the price of making old ladies think they will go to hell if they have the flu, and thus miss Mass.

That is an absurd overstatement, but you might know Catholics who would hold it. Nor is the position far off stating the fears of 'conservatives' who, after the Second Vatican Council, have seen so much bewildering change. One old priest told me that he thought John Paul II has done a fine job of teaching, that the task of the next

Pope will be to enforce that teaching. 'Enforce' is a word of the 'bad old days' for some, and for others a hope of the future.

One hope I have for this book is that you as the reader will be able to see the rules and practices in context, and in proportion. If that sounds a bit too 'liberal' to you, then reflect that it is often easier to follow instructions when you know what they mean. So let's start with a basic statement of what the Church is for, and from an impeccable source:

> Christ ... united himself with each person. The Church therefore sees its fundamental task in enabling that union to be brought about and renewed continually. The Church wishes to serve this single end: that each person may be able to find Christ, in order that Christ may walk with each person the path of life, with the power of the truth about humanity and the world that is contained in the mystery of the Incarnation and the Redemption and with the power of the love that is radiated by that truth.
>
> John Paul II, *Redemptor Hominis*, 13

A bargain

'That Christ may walk with each person the path of life.' Let's take this, and this alone, as a starting point for reflection and, leaving issues and worries aside, see what God has to say to us in it. We might find that some problems begin to look different. But there is a condition for reading on. If you agree, then let's go ahead.

Let go of what you know, especially if you are a conservative or a liberal who has all the answers. If, like the rest of us, you are merely confused or curious, take a risk. Come to God, the Father revealed in Christ, with hands empty of all but fears and loves. He will grant a context. There is absolutely no point examining God as though he is a laboratory specimen. If you wish to hear his word, you have to be prepared for the consequences. And, if you do not wish to be a Pharisee, let us begin as sinners.

PART 1

LAYING THE FOUNDATION

Chapter 1

RIGHT WAY DOWN

Let me hear your voice; for your voice is sweet and your face is beautiful.

Song of Songs 2:14

Not long ago, my father moved into a new house, a converted steading in a rather remote Scottish valley. On holiday, I helped him with some of the unpacking and decorating. The key task was to get the kitchen done, so that we could eat. In a very short time, surprisingly short, I learnt how to assemble kitchen units from flat packs. The next lesson was how to take them apart again. It was plain to me that these things were designed by warped minds, inventing devious ways of joining bits of chipboard together, and delighting in the failure of ordinary rational people to work out what had gone wrong when there were not enough bolts and screws.

Two corner units later, the truth dawned that all the bits were shaped and arranged so as to make things easy. What had looked like a confusing array of parts fell naturally into an intelligible whole if one simply followed the instructions provided. For example, the odd L-shaped bolts, far from being menacing, took away the need to make mortice joints in the wood. They meant that even I, with no experience or expertise, could assemble the units, given time, patience and a willingness to imitate the diagrams. It was a mistake even to put the pictures into words: 'put all the L-shaped bolts into the 8mm round holes at the top and bottom corners of the inside faces of the ...' The description lost clarity, added confusion. You just made the bits and pieces look like the picture provided.

It is this easy to be a Christian, to resolve any issue of faith or of practice. The hard part is learning to do it the easy way. How often, for example, have you heard or read the following?

> Come to me all you who labour and are overburdened, and I will give you rest. Shoulder my yoke and learn from me, for I am gentle and humble in heart, and you will find rest for your souls. Yes, my yoke is easy, and my burden is light.
>
> Matthew 11:28

If we could do that, there would be no problems we could not face. The trouble is that we tend to flounder around with partial ideas, half concepts, fears and anxieties, like somebody trying to assemble a kitchen unit who does not know what the different parts are for. The claim of the Gospel is very straightforward. In Jesus Christ we have our diagram; if we can configure ourselves so as to look like him then, in any situation, life will get better. Or, if it does not get any better, it will make more sense: *you will find rest for your souls*.

Such is the promise of God in Jesus. You have to decide for yourself if it is true in your life, and why it is or why it might not be. The Gospel may well be false, a delusion. But if we are to reject it, we must be sure that it is the Gospel that we reject, and not something else. If we seek to live by it, we need to know that it is truly Christ to whom we are coming. This may seem obvious, but it is important to say it, because Catholicism is so massive, so complex, and thus so misunderstood. In this chapter, let's keep things simple, and think a little about what it means to believe the Gospel.

Waving not drowning

One of the reasons English is such a rich language is that it is an amalgam of many other languages. This is especially true of so-called American English. From the fusion of Anglo-Saxon and Norman French at the turn of the first millennium we have a dual vocabulary for many things. A rich man is also wealthy; but if bereft, he is also desolate. It can cause problems, however. In talking about God, we want to talk about *faith*. That comes from the Romance or Latin side. But there is also the word *belief*. Can these be used interchangeably? In terms of grammar, no. We can say, 'I believe in God,' but not, 'I faith God.'

This draws attention to a number of meanings of the word 'belief' that need to be watched. You know it is raining, are of the opinion that it will stop soon. Belief tends to be seen as halfway between the two. It is not certain, but nor is it merely opinion. Opinion is for things we cannot really prove, whereas belief is not relinquished so easily. Such was the treatment of faith by the medieval theologians, and it has largely stuck.

Sometimes, though, people ask of any given doctrine if they have to believe it to be Catholics. This can be an unhelpful way of seeing faith: essentially as holding a number of statements to be true. If you believe propositions a, b, c, and so on, then you will go to heaven. We will come back to some difficulties in chapter 12, 'How to Disagree with the Pope'. For now, it is enough to point out that religion is not the same as a bunch of views about metaphysics and history, though these are involved in it. It is about God, about you, and about how those two relate in respect to others. This may turn out to be quite good news.

For a richer idea of what faith is about, let us look at a familiar Gospel story. Like many other stories, it is not as simple as it looks. But then, that's life.

Jesus made the disciples get into the boat and go on ahead to the other side while he would send the crowds away. After sending the crowds away he went up into the hills by himself to pray. When evening came, he was there alone, while the boat, by now far out on the lake, was battling with a heavy sea, for there was a head-wind. In the fourth watch of the night he went towards them, walking on the lake, and when the disciples saw him walking on the lake they were terrified. 'It is a ghost,' they said, and cried out in fear. But at once Jesus called out to them, saying, 'Courage! It is I! Do not be afraid.' It was Peter who answered. 'Lord,' he said, 'if it is you, tell me to come to you across the water.' 'Come,' said Jesus. Then Peter got out of the boat and started walking towards Jesus across the water, but as soon as he felt the force of the wind, he took fright and began to sink. 'Lord! Save me!' he cried. Jesus put out his hand at once and touched him. 'Man of little faith,' he said, 'why did you doubt?' And as they got into the boat, the wind dropped. The men in the boat bowed down before him and said, 'Truly, you are the Son of God.'

Matthew 14:22–33

St Peter spends much of his, time in the Gospels getting things wrong. Before Christ's arrest, he promises to follow him even to the death, but ends up denying to the authorities that he ever knew Jesus. Most people draw some consolation from this. Peter is quite like us: a real faith, but a weak faith; a real hope, but an anxious hope; a real love of Christ, but a fearful love. Christianity looks great, and even attractive, but then so difficult as well.

But let's be honest, and give Peter some credit. Would you have even got out of the boat? Perhaps you would not have got into the boat in the first place on such a stormy night? Peter errs almost always out of a misdirected enthusiasm, too much warmth. That is not something of which I can be accused very often. Perhaps you are better. But then, what are you warm about? Are you passionate in the cause of women's ordination, or for the admission of remarried divorcees to communion? Do you get hot under the collar about vacuous musical moanings in church, or fired up at the thought of young people living 'in sin'?

This is why I have laboured the point about belief not being *in the first instance* about propositions. None of these initially motivated Peter. To stretch the analogy, he did not engage in a rational process. He did not think anything like: 'Jesus is the Son of God. Faith in him can move mountains. Therefore, if I believe all that he says, I will be able to walk on water. So, off I go. Oh no, but it's very windy and the water is very wet. Surely I can't really float. Help, Lord, I'm sinking.'

In fact, in this story at any rate, Peter did not think at all. He saw and recognized Christ, and just moved. The sight of Jesus drove all from his mind, including some quite important facts. So, then, how like Peter are you? Are you so full of joy at the sight of Jesus that you forget what lies between you, what keeps you apart from him?

What made Peter disregard the wind and the waves, as well as the obvious facts about water and heavy human beings? What gave him that joy, that attraction? It was not faith, or hope, or love, but something much more interesting. It was his need, the clarity with which he felt it, the honesty with which he acknowledged it. Peter walked on water because in Christ he found someone who could and would *put out his hand and hold him*. Rather than pillory Peter for his lack of faith, we should praise him for the strength of his doubt: doubt of God, doubt of himself. Because that is where we start too, and where we will stay unless we can understand that we do not believe, we do not hope, and we do not love our Lord. If you insist that you do believe, then Jesus can do nothing for you, because you do not need him. He cannot find you if you continue to insist that you are not lost.

Maybe you think that is going a bit far. But please remember our bargain. We agreed not to be Pharisees, but sinners, because we wanted to hear and understand anew the call of Christ. If we do, then something rather marvellous happens. We receive a gift, the gift of a hopeful and loving faith. If you don't believe me, then try the Pope:

> Anyone who wishes to understand themselves thoroughly – and not just in accordance with immediate, partial, superficial and even illusory standards and measures of his being – they must with their unrest, uncertainty and even their weakness and sinfulness, with their life and death, draw near to Christ ...
>
> John Paul II, *Redemptor Hominis*, 10

So here is the only prerequisite for coming to know Jesus as your Saviour. If you want to have faith, this is the secret. Neglect all you know or don't know about God. Abandon attempts to reconcile the contradictions of the Alexandrian interpretation of the hypostatic union, or to understand transubstantiation. Forget everything except your unrest, your uncertainty, your weakness and your sinfulness. Dwell with them for as long as you can stand it. Then just suppose, as a hypothesis, that you are loved to a depth you cannot imagine. Your lover will die for you, lives for you. This takes us far beyond the merely intellectual. In the same passage, John Paul II says that

> if this profound process takes place within you, you will bear fruit not only of adoration of God, but also of deep wonder at yourself and how precious you must be in his eyes. The name for such deep amazement at your worth and dignity is the Gospel, that is to say: the Good News. It is also called Christianity.
>
> *Redemptor Hominis*, 10; slightly paraphrased

You may not find this way of working very helpful as an immediate experience. But the Pope's point stands that faith begins in a sense of how much we need, and then astonishment at the suggestion that Jesus is prepared to fulfil that need. It is good theology as well as a way of praying. If you disagree, try living without love. Or, from God's point of view, try compelling someone else to live without love (except *don't*, of course!).

Peter fails because he stops at doubt. His need brings panic; he *must* cross over to Christ. He ignores the truth that Jesus is coming to him, just as he ignores the comparatively irrelevant Archimedean principle (he'll sink). But there is no necessity to leave the boat, because when Jesus arrives the wind will drop and the waves become calm. Don't just do something, sit there!

This is the truly amazing part of the Gospel, and the easiest to forget: that God moves long before we do. Before we can call, he is there. Before we can repent, he has forgiven. We will see this again in later chapters, so I will leave its expansion to those applications. For now, it simply means that there is no place to which Jesus cannot follow you. The reason is that, because of his love for you, there is no place where he does not want to follow you, just to be with you, and to draw you back to the Father.

Man of little faith, why did you doubt? Doubt everything you like – yourself, your strength, your worthiness, even God and his love. Faith does not erase those doubts, because they are truth, truth about us. Faith adds another, contradictory fact, a fact about God: the Lord is coming to save.

What about the creed?

If this is what faith is about, then it shows us how important the Creed is, and what the teaching of the Church's magisterium is for. Doctrines are vital because they attempt to encapsulate and apply the content of the Gospel. They derive their significance from the personal contact with Christ which is that content; the wonder or amazement of which John Paul II has spoken. This can be demonstrated from the simple experience of the Church's history and life. For example, as we will see below, the only way to express adequately in human language the intensity with which Jesus gives himself to us in the Eucharist is to talk of eating his Body and drinking his Blood; and to mean that, literally. Less controversially, when discussing the nature of Christ, the early theologians insisted that Christ was fully human, because 'what was not assumed by God in Christ was not saved', and the Christian hope is of salvation of the whole human person.

The Pope and the bishops have the task of interpreting human need and divine response in each age and all circumstances. This is a sufficiently daunting commission to encourage one to have sympathy with them. Even more so, when one realizes that they do so, and can do so, only in union with the whole Body of Christ; including you and me.

This tells us, further, how to interpret the Church's teaching. Any given doctrine is not the result of speculation, but is forced on us to express our faith. So, in turn, we say that we believe the doctrine, that is, say it is true, because the doctrine says what we mean by putting our faith in God, revealed in Christ. Conversely, pick a doctrine, and we can try to work out what it really means in the light of the Gospel it expresses. Take murder. The Church agrees with many others that in most instances it is wrong to kill. Why? Because each human life has an equal value in God's sight. Conversely, I am loved by God in and for myself, regardless of how tall I am or what I do. Hence, you are too. So it would not be consistent with the good news of my own life to take yours.

If only life were that simple all the time. We are nearly ready to tackle some real problems. But first, we need a few doctrines to provide ammunition, protection and shorthand. In the next few chapters, we shall look more closely at the figure approaching across the storm-tossed waters. Who is he, and what does he have to do with us?

Chapter 2

WORD MADE FLESH

Our God comes, he keeps silence no longer.

Psalm 50:3, Grail translation

In this chapter, we are going to look at the central doctrine of the Christian faith, the doctrine of the Incarnation. The essential idea is that Jesus Christ was both truly God and truly Man. As we approach this doctrine we are faced with a number of difficulties. One is the seeming contradiction in saying that the same person can be omnipotent (divine) and hungry (human). Another has arisen more recently but is just as acute – that Jesus was (or should I say 'is'; that's another problem!) a man and not a woman. The Incarnation seems to feed into Christian chauvinism, the devaluing of women, and, historically, probably has done so.

Once again, I ask you to take it on trust that these issues have resolutions, and suggest that the way forward is not to keep banging our heads on intractables or waving a number of political flags in either direction. Let's try to get to the heart of the matter, and then see. Having put down any weapons, let's listen to a story from the Mass, slightly edited.

You formed us in your own likeness, and set us over the whole world, to serve you, our Creator, and to rule over all creatures. Even when we disobeyed you and lost your friendship, you did not abandon us to the power of death, but helped us all to seek and find you. Again and again, you offered us a covenant, and through the prophets taught us to hope for salvation.

Roman Missal, n. 118, Eucharistic Prayer IV

We can read this in a number of ways. One approach is to take it personally. We all have in us a sense of being and of reason and love, which is the likeness to God. We also have a sense of difference from plants and other animals, a sense of understanding and control. We also have the sad knowledge of what we have done with that sense and the power that comes with it. You also know in yourself, if you are honest, ways and examples of lost love and friendship, instances in which you are not what you could be, best intentions frustrated.

But there is also hope, which gets you up in the morning, makes you try again; possibilities of reform, of forgiveness. Either of these senses, of sin and of grace, can be to the fore or fade out of sight from time to time, but recognizing the idea of them is enough for now. A very good way of praying is to take that text above, put it in the first person singular, 'I', and the present tense: *you do not abandon me to the power of death*.

The story is also a history. It is told, mostly, in the documents that make up the Old Testament, the first, and longer, half of the Christian Bible. On the face of it, some may think that there's little point in having the Old Testament. If you open it at random, there is a fair chance you will find something incomprehensible or irrelevant. Some of it is downright irreligious, or even shocking; for example, the ethnic cleansing of Palestine in the name of God, described in the books of Joshua and Judges. There were quite influential movements in the first years of Christianity which said the Old Testament should be ditched. Not only was it disedifying and even scandalous in parts, but with the coming of Christ it had become, literally, history, to be replaced by the New. The main group were called Marcionites, after their leader, and they failed because they were discredited by a far bigger mistake, of which more in a moment.

But there is something reassuring about the realism of the Old Testament. It has three main sections: the history and law books, such as I Kings or Exodus; the Prophets, such as Isaiah or Jeremiah; and the 'writings', a miscellaneous collection including the Psalms, Proverbs and the Song of Songs. There is virtually no human aspiration, hope, virtue, failure, betrayal, emotion or drama that cannot be found in there somewhere. Early monks used to make the same claim of the Psalms alone. Once noticed, this fact is significant. There would be something odd about a religion that addressed only what is true and noble in us. Not just odd, but totally abstract, even useless. Think back to Peter, and his raw need for God. That need comes from sin, from weakness, from a damaging history. The Old Testament tells your story and mine in the form of the story and prayers of Israel.

That is as far as we have got up to now; the realization of doubt and emptiness, and the instinct that there is an alternative. Plus the not altogether comfortable hypothesis that we are loved by a God who is about to do something about all three. Here we have the full and richer purpose of the Old Testament in Christian scripture and life, expressed in the continuation of the prayer with which we began:

> Father, you so loved the world that in the fullness of time you sent your only Son to be our Saviour. He was conceived by the power of the Holy Spirit, and born of the Virgin Mary, a man like us in all things but sin. To the poor he proclaimed the good news of salvation, to prisoners freedom, and to those in sorrow, joy.
>
> *Roman Missal*, Eucharistic Prayer IV

The Old Testament tells the story of the preparation in history for this event, in the calling of Israel to be the people within which a saviour for the world could be born and reared. We can read of the slow formation and revelation of religious and other traditions from which the 'good news of salvation' could be derived. For, if one stops to think about it, the message of salvation could not be proclaimed without actions and words. Further, words and actions need a context, a time and a place, and an audience rooted in that context to become comprehensible. They also need a context within which to become compelling.

It is vital to recall the kind of context that is meant here. It is not simply a matter of an agreed set of words, and a grammar for what they mean in combination. Here is an example to try to indicate what the 'extra' element is. It is from a prayer spoken by a prophet eight centuries before Christ:

> With shepherd's crook lead your people to pasture, the flock that is your heritage, living confined in a forest with meadow land all around. Let them pasture in Bashan and Gilead as in the days of old. As in the days when you came out of Egypt grant us to see wonders ...

Once more have pity on us, tread down our faults, to the bottom of
the sea throw all our sins.

Micah 7:14–15, 19

I defy anyone with insight into themselves not to empathize with
the hope of that prayer. This is the context I mean, the gradual
forming of human history to expect and receive God's response to
our plight. Jesus had a simple proclamation, that in his life the time
was fulfilled, and the response had begun. 'Today these words are
being fulfilled, even as you listen' (Luke 4:21).

Watch my lips

In the course of this chapter I have left quite a few hostages of some
importance. The last extract from the Fourth Eucharistic Prayer
mentions the virgin birth, the Trinity and social justice, among
other things. There was also a rash promise to explain the
Incarnation. The latter is really quite simple in the Old Testament
context. For we have here the issue of *how* God can give us his message. Again and again he sends prophets, and tugs at our hope; to
little avail. The issue is not just historical, since the salvation history closely mirrors our everyday experience of up and down (or,
even worse, just *along* a flat, uninspiring road). What can he do, to
tell us of his love?

An image: my attempts to build a corner unit. There is a need to
assemble it so that there will be supper, and also an instinct that I
can assemble the thing. It looks easy, and a muddled process of
sticking things together results two times out of five in an imitation
of the real thing. There is a gradual process of revelation as the various bits and planks acquire a meaning and purpose that I can
understand, though much remains mysterious. Then a pattern is
provided to copy. So there is the humanity of Jesus, one like us in
all things but sin.

Here the analogy breaks down, and we move into the realm of
faith. But it is not the open credulity or frenzied legalism kind of
faith. In Christ we have our pattern and model. On its own, this just
makes it worse. Already we had such things in the law and the
prophets, and that did not help. In Peter's terms (see chapter 1),
Jesus is still far off across a forbidding ocean of divine demand and
human failure. One uniquely good man is not enough to express

God's message; so much is proved by what we did and do to that one good man and his memory. What else is needed?

> In the beginning was the Word: the Word was with God, and the Word was God ... All that came to be had life in him and that life is our light, a light that shines in the dark, a light that darkness could not over-power. The Word was made flesh, he lived among us, and we saw his glory, the glory that is his as the only Son of the Father, full of grace and truth ... From his fullness we have, all of us, received, grace upon grace. No one has ever seen God; it is the only Son, who is nearest to the Father's heart, who has made him known.
>
> John 1:1, 3–5, 14, 16–18

After centuries of trying to tell us, God the Father decided to show us. Here is the incredible fact at the centre of our faith, that God himself has come to save in Christ. It is incredible on two levels. First, theology: what is the difference between Son and Father, why is the Son called 'Word', how are they both God, how can God become man, etc. These are all easy compared to the second level: why would God want to become one of us, hopeless, little betray-ing things? What a risk, and what a failure, because we did and do not receive him, but slay him on the Cross and in ourselves and each other. Why? We already have the answer, but it is almost too deeply threatening.

> God loved the world so much that he gave his only Son, so that everyone who believes in him may not be lost but may have eternal life. For God sent his Son into the world not to condemn the world, but so that through him the world might be saved.
>
> John 3:16–17

The Incarnation cannot be explained, because it is wholly gratu-itous. There is no reason on earth for it, apart from you. But we can understand a little what it implies. Remember the Marcionites? Their key fault was to be associated with a group which could not accept that the Word had become flesh. Christ did not really hunger, sleep or suffer. He only pretended to do so, in order to teach us various things, such as the value of a noble steadfastness in the face of difficulty. He did not rise from the dead, because he did not die; he only seemed to. This suggestion is called docetism, from a Greek word meaning 'to seem', and the group tend to be called Gnostics, because they thought that Jesus had imparted a saving knowledge (*gnosis*, in Greek). This knowledge was like a set of passwords that would lead us to God past all obstacles, earthly and demonic.

What Gnostics could not stand was matter, especially bodies. Real reality, they would say, is spiritual, untainted by the flesh. There is no need to spell out the baleful influence of such thinking on Christian life, and sometimes even doctrine. Jesus said once, 'the spirit is willing, but the flesh is weak' (Matthew 26:42). The Gnostics went further and said that the flesh is bad, evil. Some went so far as to say that there are two powers: God, who made the soul, and a wicked demi-god who trapped us in flesh.

This is not Christian, and we shall see why in later chapters. The Incarnation affirms once and for all the Genesis message that the creation is good, is loved by God. The aim of Christ is not to free us *from* matter, but to free us *for* it. It is we who are alienated from ourselves, spirit and body. But, 'if the Spirit of him who raised Jesus from the dead is living in you, then he who raised Jesus from the dead will give life to your mortal bodies through his Spirit living in you' (Romans 8:11).

The reason Gnostics found the Old Testament so difficult was that it is so earthy, so everyday. Pots and pans were not just boring, but revolting to them. The Incarnation says the opposite, that God delights to be with us so much that he became one of us. The Second Vatican Council put it like this (the full passage is given at the end of the chapter):

> Christ the Lord, who is the 'image of the invisible God', worked with human hands, he thought with a human mind. He acted with a human will, and with a human heart he loved.
>
> *Gaudium et Spes*, 22; the scriptural quotation is from St Paul, Colossians 1:15

In Christ, the invisible God found an image. God was invisible because he is beyond our imagining, but also because we have forgotten what he looks like. We have lost the image in ourselves. In Jesus, the words of God took flesh, in a practical demonstration. Our assumptions tend to play this down; we assume that at any moment, the divinity was on top. But to take the Incarnation seriously is to say that Jesus could have died at the age of four from yellow fever.

Has it ever struck you how little the Gospels tell us about the life of Christ? There have been plenty of novels and films to fill the gap: most of those in the first few centuries were written by Gnostics, silly stories about Jesus zapping his childhood friends (wish I could), and so were rejected by the Church. In the genuine scriptures of the New Testament we have two nativity stories, and that is it until Jesus is about thirty. There is only one exception, in Luke's Gospel, where Jesus goes missing on a visit to Jerusalem, and is found in the Temple, giving the learned priests a run for their money. It is a rather charming picture of an ordinary family event: a lost child, panic, reproaches and answering back. The Gospels tell us nothing of the boyhood of the Saviour because he was just another kid.

Maybe you find all this shocking. It is indeed shocking, but because it is the full revelation of God's love, not because it is blasphemy. If Jesus was not fully man, then he did not show us what *humanity* could be. If he did not live as we do, then God has no interest in our lives. If he did not die, then our own deaths are the end, there will be no rising. God stands, unruffled, on the stormy lake and taunts us with advice on how to bail out the water.

But that is how we think, not how God thinks, which is just as well. So now we have the Son of God and us, all in the same boat. From this we can come to understand most of what we want to know about being Catholic.

It is only in the mystery of the Word made flesh that the mystery of man truly becomes clear. Christ the Lord, Christ the new Adam, in the very revelation of the mystery of the Father and of his love, fully reveals man to himself and brings to light his most high calling. He who is the 'image of the invisible God', is himself the perfect man who has restored in the children of Adam that likeness to God which had been disfigured ever since the first sin. Human nature, by the very fact that it was assumed, not absorbed, in him, has been raised in us also to a dignity beyond compare. For, by his incarnation, he, the Son of God, has in a certain way united himself with each man. He worked with human hands, he thought with a human mind. He acted with a human will, and with a human heart he loved.

Second Vatican Council, *Gaudium et Spes*, 22

It is time to say what that might mean for us, and for him. First, however, there is a possible apprehension that needs to be cleared up.

Chapter 3

WILL GOD PUNISH YOU?

Death was not God's doing.

Wisdom 1:13

From time to time you hear people say that the problem with the Church now is that nobody believes in sin any more. It has all become a sickly soup of love and forgiveness. What about the wrath of God? What about the fires of hell and of purgatory? Surely, if you do bad, you are punished, and if you do good, you are rewarded. Justice, love and peace are all very well, but the world also contains oppression, hate and violence. We do wrong either to ourselves, or to each other.

Such people have a point. If the Gospel is all about things going right, and people full of Christian charity and nothing else, then it has very little to do with any of us. The tendency to think that God forgives everything really, in the end, is to an extent connected with wish-fulfilment, the desire to live in a perfect world, undisturbed. But, on the other hand, it seems strange, to say the least, that the God who is love might condemn anyone he has made to eternal and final suffering in punishment for offences which, in the perspective of infinite goodness, are maybe not that big.

Not so fast

On this question, Jesus has a very unwelcome thing to say. His view is almost impossible to explain away; though, of course, that has not stopped people from trying. When you read it, you can see the temptation to marshal the technology of literary and historical criticism to prove that Jesus did not actually say it. But I think his statement, grim as it looks, has much to tell us about the full richness of the Good News. It is worth taking it on the chin, and examining ourselves and our reaction to it. Here it is, from St Mark's account:

> I tell you solemnly, all men's sins will be forgiven, and all their blasphemies; but let anyone blaspheme against the Holy Spirit and he will never have forgiveness; he is guilty of an eternal sin.
>
> Mark 3:28–30

Mark tells us that Jesus said this because some scribes were attributing his miracles to demonic possession. The statement might almost confirm their suspicions. There is, according to Jesus, a special reserved sin that will not be forgiven, no matter how sorry you are, and how much you repent. Worried? You should be. For it seems that after baptism, and a sacramental life of eucharist and reconciliation, you can finally and truly blow it. Murders, genocides, can all be forgiven; but let anyone speak against the Holy Spirit, and he, or she, is lost for ever. God is more touchy about his honour than about the lives of his children.

At least, however, we can be assured that the Christian tradition does contain some tough and uncompromising claims about sin and punishment. It may also be clear from your own reaction to the text why hell, damnation and sin have so dropped out of the contemporary religious vocabulary. Perhaps, for example, you are the rare person who reads the above saying with warm feelings of approval and agreement. Presumably you do not feel it applies to you! Maybe you think Jesus has said this to try and spur us into repentance and a safely good life, in case we fall into the dreadful pit. So, are we meant to live Christian lives motivated by fear of punishment alone, and a scrupulous, ritualistic fetish for moral cleanliness? This may be true, though I hope not! It is certainly not the Gospel as expounded in the old Penny Catechism:

> God made me to know him, love him and serve him in this world, and to be happy with him for ever in the next.
>
> Question 2

The 's' word

If you really know God, you know that he is God, not The Godfather. St Benedict, in his *Rule for Monks*, describes coming to know God as a growth from servile fear to the love of sons and daughters, the perfect love that casts out fear. For him, it is a growth in humility. This virtue has two parts. The first is the recognition of weakness and sin within us. The second is the realization that goodness and beauty is there too. Each part is useless without the other. On its own, the first is false modesty, or unctuous hypocrisy. The second without the first is conceit, a comforting internal deafness to what we do not want to know.

Both parts together involve living in the truth, the exclusion of false gloom or over-optimism. It is also the only way to understand how Jesus' preaching of the gospel of repentance is good news to us.

> If we say we have no sin in us, we are deceiving ourselves and refusing to admit the truth; but if we acknowledge our sins, then God who is faithful and just will forgive our sins and purify us from everything that is wrong.
>
> 1 John 1:8–9

For a Christian, talk of sin is immediately the acknowledgement of grace and forgiveness because 'what proves that God loves us is that Christ died for us while we were still sinners' (Romans 5:8). On the other hand, talk of God's love makes no sense without at least some sense of our darker side, the things in us that he wants to heal and change so that he can truly share with us love for love.

Hence, fear of punishment cannot be the fundamental motivation for a mature Christian. But there is another way of taking Jesus' words about an eternal sin with immediate approval. If you look around the world, there is plenty going on that should surely be unforgivable. It does not seem right that the likes of Hitler or Stalin should jump any queues into heaven ahead of, say, those millions who were killed trying to stop the evils perpetrated by them. If God waves a wand or puts a blind over his eyes with truly wicked people, and sees Christ instead of them and so lets them into eternal bliss, then this makes his love for you and me, who struggle on and do as little harm as we can, rather unreal. Salvation becomes like a debased coinage, without value because it has no cost. It must be correct, then, that a person can put him- or herself beyond the possibility of forgiveness. It is like a relationship fractured to the degree that 'I'm sorry' can no longer heal.

So who gets it?

But, if you are inclined to agree with this, be careful. Jesus has another uncomfortable truth to tell us:

> Two men went up to the Temple to pray, one a Pharisee, and the other a tax collector. The Pharisee stood there and said this prayer to himself, 'I thank you, God, that I am not grasping, unjust, adulterous like the rest of mankind, and particularly that I am not like this tax collector here. I fast twice a week; I pay tithes on all I get.' The tax collector stood some distance away, not daring even to raise his eyes to heaven; but he beat his breast and said, 'God, be merciful to me, a sinner.' This man, I tell you, went home again at rights with God; the other did not. For everyone who exalts himself will be humbled, but the man who humbles himself will be exalted.
>
> Luke 18:9–14

The point at present is that, even if the tax collector had not said his truly humble prayer, the Pharisee is at fault. His prayer is superficially humble, in that he does thank God for the gifts within him. But it is only half the truth. In fact he uses his virtue as a condemnation of the tax collector. Any demand on our part that God be fair, and punish those evil-doers as they deserve, either condemns us to the same fate (be honest!) or puts us in the shoes of the Pharisee, whose prayer of thanksgiving was counted as sin. So maybe Hitler is in the hottest part of hell. But it is not for us to say that; unless, perhaps, you want to join him.

Let us assume, therefore, a certain resistance to the idea of an eternal sin, and move forward to what Jesus might mean by it. The idea itself is not hard to understand. A woman discovers that her husband has been having an affair with her best friend for the last ten years. How does she react? What is the next step? It depends, of course, on her, her husband, and their relationship. She might just walk out. She might confront him and threaten divorce unless he stays faithful to her. She may file for divorce and seek a punitive financial settlement. She might take his shotgun and murder them both. She may do nothing at all, turn a blind eye, or even collude for the sake of children, reputation or security. Most people, though, would understand if she felt that life could not be as it was before, however much he repents or makes it up to her. A basic trust has gone, and the slate will never again be clean.

We have nearly all had close relationships that have broken up – often for some reason we do not really know – or just drifted apart. Young couples sometimes insist that they are splitting up in order to 'stay good friends'. Sometimes they can, but usually they don't. Most of us have had the horrible experience of saying something that really lost somebody's trust; even without meaning to, the wounding thing is out. It can take a long time to rebuild, and the foundation is never what it was, wish as we may. Human life is full of eternal sins, clocks that will not go back. In contemporary Britain, some criminal offences are eternal in the sense that once committed, they can never be forgotten. Most people agree, for example, that paedophiles may be punished for seeking to work with children. Killers released early on parole sometimes have to be protected from the vengeful public. It seems that human society, to protect itself, has to cast some of its members into the outer darkness.

If the idea of an eternal sin makes some sense, the claim that in the sight of God there are points of no return perhaps does not. Take the maltreated and deceived wife. What if she had a perfect love for her husband? She might know him very well, understand some fact of his character or history that made him unable to cope with fidelity. She might realize how much he needed her there to return to. She might reflect that no husband is ideal, and put the blame on her friend. In other words, she might do all the things we would expect of the loving Father. God is love. He sees our weakness, understands its roots, knows what we can and cannot help. He notes our attempts to repent, and stands, like the father in the parable of the Prodigal Son, on the road waiting for us. He knows we are fallen, none better, and he knows we are tempted by a former angel of light. And did he not wipe it all away in the death of his Son?

All shall have prizes?

This is a childish way of thinking, precisely what Jesus wants us to abandon. It is like the mad queen in Lewis Carroll's story who exclaims after a game, 'All have won, and all shall have prizes!' Suppose our offended lady does all those things, and puts up with the errant behaviour, while seeking always to draw her husband from it. He is still unfaithful, and he is still, despite all protestations, someone who has been unfaithful. But because she is a good lady, on one view, she treats him still as if he were entirely hers, heart and soul. Some people think that this is what God does with us. He looks at our sins and instead of the guilty sinner, sees his Son. He counts us as righteous; this is the 'good news' that God loves us always despite our sins. He casts them into a bottomless sea, and forgets them.

So let us imagine heaven on that basis. We all have the full vision of God, we live in some kind of state surrounded by the light and love of the Trinity; all is for us. We are still sinners, of course, but that is all paid for. We are like compulsive gamblers, and God has agreed to pay all our gambling debts, content that we are having fun. Would this be eternal blessedness, paradise? It sounds to me to be more like this world, and what we have made of it. Or maybe just hell on earth. Sheep may safely graze, and wolves may safely prey on them. The lion lies down with the lamb and eats it for lunch. The infant plays over the viper's hole and is bitten. The Father takes no notice; his children make of each other a living torment, and the God of love says that all is well. I will not labour this point, but simply recall what we are really promised:

> The wolf lives with the lamb, the panther lies down with the kid, calf and lion cub feed together with a little boy to lead them. The cow and the bear make friends, their young lie down together. The lion eats straw like the ox. The infant plays over the cobra's hole; into the viper's lair the young child puts his hand. They do no hurt, no harm, on all my holy mountain, for the country is filled with the knowledge of the Lord, as the waters swell the sea.
>
> Isaiah 11:6–9

Jesus Christ does not offer a game of 'let's pretend'. He offers you the real possibility of being freed from your sins. In which case, there is the real possibility that you will refuse his offer. He will not turn the blind eye, for your sake. His promise is to do what no human alone can do, which is to restore the basic trust that was lost, to make all creation new, so as to have you back with him, whole and entire. In this light, we can understand what Jesus is talking about. The eternal sin, blasphemy against the Holy Spirit, is not a stone cast at the honour of a touchy God. It is your refusal of his offer to give you his love, to teach you how to love him, and your neighbour, let alone your enemies; the offer to fill you with his Holy Spirit.

God will not punish you. But you might; in fact, you do. I'll try to explain in the next chapter.

Chapter 4

A BETTER IDEA

Has the Lord lost patience? Is that his way?

Micah 2:7

Of course, it would be very easy for God to punish us. He is the Creator of all things, sustaining in being all that is seen and even more that is unseen. At any moment he could destroy you, rewrite history so that you never were. He could do things undreamed of by even the most expert ethnic cleanser. It would be equally easy for him to free you from your sins, make you perfect, just like that. But he is not going to do either of those things, obvious as they might seem. He has a better idea altogether, though much more difficult and perhaps impossible:

> Such is the richness of the grace he has showered on us in all wisdom and insight. He has let us know the mystery of his purpose, the hidden plan he so kindly made in Christ from the beginning to act upon when the times had run their course to an end.
>
> Ephesians 1:8–9

So, what is this plan, and why is it hidden? The two questions have one answer. Let us think for a moment about God as the Creator of heaven and earth. It is hard to imagine what this means. We are familiar with making things, be they kitchen units or works of art and poetry. Parents have the most sublime experience of all in the creation of a completely new person. When we create, it involves assembling or rearranging bits of matter, or thoughts. God, in contrast, created everything out of nothing. This involves two ideas.

First, God started it all off: 'Let there be light', and so on. On its own, however, this idea does not capture much. God would be like the Queen, in the United Kingdom, smashing a bottle against a ship to launch it, blessing all who sail in it, and that's that.

The full truth is rather less comfortable, because it brings God very, very near. You do not need the Queen to launch the ship, though she does do it very well. It could be anyone sober enough to heft the bottle in the right direction. It could also be a machine suitably programmed. Or, why bother with an intervention? Just let the ship slide. In the same way, God the Creator need not be at all like the Father revealed in his Word by the Holy Spirit. It could be any kind of god with sufficient strength to give the big push. Or, the universe might just have happened. The notion of a Creator might just be a useful myth to take us beyond the boundaries of the language of science, the kind of confusion that comes from perplexing questions like 'what was there before there was anything?'

The idea of the Christian doctrine of creation is this: behind every happening, every thing, every thought, every action, all movements, is the creating power of God. In gaps between nanoseconds, he sustains it in being. There is only one force in the world, which is the action of God. Nothing happens otherwise.

Hold on, though. Aren't we free beings, with choice? What about all the catastrophes and natural disasters; am I saying that God wills those? Am I saying that God is responsible for evil actions by tyrants and people like us? In asking these questions, we are coming to understand what sin is. A sinful act is not sinful primarily because it offends God, or because it infringes some abstract law code. It is sinful because it is an exercise of the power to act, given by God, in an evil way, a way that counts against God's purpose in creating us.

Philosophers have argued for centuries – and there is no reason for them to stop – about how it is possible for an all-powerful Creator to have made free creatures. Surely in some remote way, he still has control. This is the nasty bit that hurts. There is nothing in creation that can withstand the power of God, except for one thing, which is a human being saying 'no'. Why? Because that is how God made it. For some reason, known only to himself, he wanted to make little beings that would accept his love and love him in return. So he gave us the ability to move, act and think for ourselves. If God were like us, he might wish he had not bothered.

Another doctrine

It is from thinking like this, however, that we get a glimpse of the inner reality of God. The argument is tricky, and largely unconvincing, because the subject is too big. Nobody expects to be able to divide one by zero, and so we should not be surprised at the mystery and complexity of the doctrine of the Trinity. It is just trying to do what every doctrine does: express in intelligible sentences something that cannot be said, but that our need tells us to be so. Before I state the doctrine, a short passage from the writings of John Paul II illustrates the starting point:

> Man cannot live without love. He remains a being which is incomprehensible for himself, his life is senseless, if love is not revealed to him, if he does not encounter love, if he does not experience it and make it his own, if he does not participate intimately in it.
>
> *Redemptor Hominis*, 10

Mothers and fathers have a particular insight into this truth, that we find fullness of life in giving life, in nurturing it, and in setting it free. The question here is *why* we are like that. God could have made little things that would freely love him in an one-to-one way. I love God, you love God, she loves God ... isolated cells of devotion.

But I love you, too (quite easy, really, if we have not met!); and you love so-and-so, and he loves you, or loves you not. Once you think of it, this is a staggering fact, the most important thing about human beings. The ancient philosophers used to say 'man is a political animal', meaning that we are intrinsically, and by nature, interactive in relation to others. If you have never thought about that, think about it now. Nor is it simply true of humanity; the whole creation is promiscuously interactional, though maybe only we have the ability to choose it, or resist it. It need not have been so, except that

> God said, 'Let us make man in our own image, in the likeness of ourselves, and let them be masters of the fish of the sea, the birds of heaven, the cattle, all the wild beasts and all the reptiles that crawl upon the earth.' God created man in the image of himself, in the image of God he created him, male and female he created them.
>
> Genesis 1:26–27

The author of Genesis was so struck by our relational nature that he went as far as can be gone, and said that we are so because God is so, and he made us so because he wanted us to be like him in love. In our nature is found a reflection of the nature of God. A shorthand idea is needed to express what is meant by something relational by nature with a power to choose. If we call this entity a 'person', then we have acquired the first vital concept for expressing a Trinitarian faith. God is personal in this sense. We know this because we are persons, but by creation, and hence by the will of an interactive Creator.

The second concept follows rather less obviously. I have suggested that creation need not have been interactional at all. It could have been like a tall building divided into one-room flats, each one with a window to the east. We could each have been in different rooms, all looking at the sun, but without awareness of each other, or any means to relate to each other, even if we wanted to. The ancient idea of man as the image of God can then be pressed further. 'Male and female he created them.' Humanity is not totally expressed by just the men or just the women, it is a plurality as well as a unity. Nature did not have to be divisible into partitions: we could all have been androgynous, or even non-sexual in nature. That stamp came from God. The Creator is a unity and a plurality.

One can go further than this still. The image of God, a humanity that is male and female, is part of the interactivity in all of creation. It is not just that men love God and women love God. Human persons were created also to love each other. In the love between a man and a woman, they can give life, share with God in creating a new person. A traditional description of the Holy Spirit comes from this way of thinking: he is the *vinculum amoris*, the chain of love between Father and Son. Again, we reflect our Creator; two distinct types of person, and their love for each other, giving rise to creation of life.

Be warned that it is very easy indeed to talk complete rubbish about the Trinity. And it is all rather difficult, even impossible, to understand (and hence to explain!) Like all other doctrines, we are putting into clumsy human words something revealed in Christ, and foreshadowed in the Old Testament. Getting the formulation true to the Christian experience of salvation took many centuries and, sadly, much controversy. If confused, we can take refuge in the

Creed that was produced, and which we still say each Sunday. But the doctrine of the Trinity, that God is one God in three Persons, is not a speculation. It comes from making sense of what Christ has done for us, which he himself expressed as a command to baptize 'in the name of the Father and of the Son and of the Holy Spirit' (Matthew 28:19).

The cunning plan

If you are feeling completely lost, that is not necessarily bad. Remember that we are awash anyway in the boat on the stormy sea, and have just been joined by Jesus. It is time to say what God's better idea for us might be. The aim is entirely simple and can be put in a very few words. Nothing does better than the special formula from the Third Eucharistic Prayer which we use at funerals:

> We hope to share in your glory when every tear will be wiped away. On that day we shall see you, our God, as you are. We shall become like you and praise you for ever through Christ our Lord, from whom all good things come.

God's solution to our needs and troubles is to restore us to his image. We need to think a little about the problems he faces in doing this. The immediate one is sin. But what is sin? You might have been brought up on lists of sins, some of them attractively mysterious. Don't lie, don't be rude, don't hate, don't commit adultery. All of these are indeed sinful, but the true nature of sin is something deeper. It is not simply that God gets angry if you do or say the wrong thing. Sin, fundamentally, is a refusal to relate to God.

No matter how much he loves us, he can give us nothing if we will not accept it. The consequences of this are dire. Imagine a human family in which all the people have decided that the mother is out to poison them. Food is not safe if it is given by her, but it is all right if it is taken for yourself. So each member has to grab what they want for themselves, and as early in the cooking process as possible so that it is not too poisonous. The result is a considerable amount of indigestion and stomach ache, the personal consequences of sin. In addition, the brothers and sisters come to distrust each other, each wishing to get the food first, and never sure if the others are not tricking them. Life becomes, in the words of the philosopher Thomas Hobbes, 'nasty, brutish and short'. Here we have the social consequences of sin, the way a personal refusal of God spreads to a refusal of others. In the end, as more children are born into the household, they pick up without choice the habits of their parents and other relations. We have a fallen society with no hope of redemption within itself.

Here is one part of the redemption in Christ, the teaching and example which reveals the love of God, whose full depth is shown in the sacrifice of the Cross. He is like someone coming into the dysfunctional family who dares to eat food from the mother's hand. But in order for the example to persuade, he has to be like them. There is no use having an exemplar whom we suspect of being immune to the poison. This is why the docetic Gnostics mentioned in chapter 2 were so dangerously wrong when they thought that God could not really have become human in Jesus, that there must have been some special 'get-out' clause or immunity for Christ. It is the same point that lies behind the temptation of Jesus in the desert: 'If you are the Son of God, turn this stone into a loaf' (Luke 4:4). Precisely because he is the Son of God, Jesus was prepared to lay his power aside so as to convince us of his love.

But sin goes deeper than that. Traditionally, the Church has talked about Original Sin, an idea which is understandably unpopular. The story is that the first sin of Adam and Eve was passed down all the generations as a hereditary curse, rather in the same way as big ears or a snub nose like mine. Theologians, especially St Augustine, noted the rage of tiny infants when disappointed of food or attention, and saw this as a mark of the fatal inheritance. But once it was realized that Adam and Eve may not have existed as such, the doctrine began to lose credibility. Nobody would put much research money into a quest for a putative 'sin' gene in human cells.

The language surrounding original sin may not hold much water any longer, but the central idea, the faith the doctrine attempts to express, has something going for it. Anyone who has undergone any form of psychotherapy discovers how basic and elemental are some of our destructive impulses. We learn more each day about the subtle interactions of genes and environments, behaviour and cognition. If you think that is all hocus-pocus, then I would point to the fact that very few of us get close to imitating Christ. We may start to take God's love, but what do we do with it then? Take the Sermon on the Mount: 'be perfect as your heavenly

Father is perfect' (Matthew 5:48). How are you doing? How much longer will you need? Our fallen state is a universal experience.

The radical Christian message is about how deep that fall has gone. We know this because we know how far God has gone in Christ to restore us to his image. The full damage of sin happens on the level of our basic nature. This is the basic content of the doctrine of Original Sin. All of us are damaged in nature, and pass that on. We know this, because the Word became flesh to rescue us. The remedy is on the same scale and level as the disease.

One way to put it is like this. Our nature is relational, we are persons. In denying ourselves the love of God, we deny ourselves the material with which to love each other. In doing this, we block off part of God's creative love from the whole world, as though we are standing in each other's light causing mini-eclipses. The love which most reflects God's, that of woman and man creating a child, is also affected, and thus there is a lack in the creative power passed on by them. It is like a dry field. Each of us is standing holding an umbrella, so that no matter how much it rains, the field remains parched. It may as well be drought. After a while, weedy, malnourished seedlings give rise to malnourished plants. That is what we have done to ourselves, to each other and to the whole creation. And so we become imperfect copies of the image of God.

What happens in Christ is that God takes on our nature. So what? So two things. First, human nature is exalted by the exchange. As the Vatican II passage already quoted makes clear, 'Human nature, by the fact that it was assumed, not absorbed, in him, has been raised in us also to a dignity beyond compare' (*Gaudium et Spes*, 22). For the first time in many years, there is a human being living in love with the Father. Jesus relates fully to the Father, so he can relate fully to other human beings. Because our nature is relational, connecting us all together in chains of love or of hate, Jesus' nature affects the rest of us. In him, the human and divine meet in amity and in union, and so if we relate to Jesus, we also relate to the Father. One such relationship can begin to leaven the whole world, because of the fact that we are all interacting across space and time. That is our shared nature, now shared with him.

But secondly, a human being has at last said a full 'yes' to God. This is not just an example, it is an opening of the world to the power of the Creator. It is also a 'yes' said by the Son of God, a loving return of love for love that is the Holy Spirit unleashed on the creation to mend and to heal. The purpose of creation is at last fulfilled and man and God are made one. Nor is this simply a unity at a level where nothing goes wrong. It is easy to live in love when all is rosy and bright. But Jesus plumbs the full depths of human misery, as well as sharing our joys. For this reason, the Cross has central importance in Christianity. Note, as well, what love it is of which we are speaking. On the Cross the Father and Son exchange the love of the Trinity; it is this image to which we are restored. Our life, from now, can be part of the life of God. To paraphrase St Paul:

> Out of the Father's infinite glory, he has offered you the power, through his Holy Spirit, for your hidden self to grow strong, so that Christ may live in your hearts through faith, and then, planted on love and built on love you will with all the saints have strength to grasp the breadth and the length, the height and the depth; until, knowing the love of Christ, which is beyond all knowledge, you are filled with the utter fullness of God.
>
> Ephesians 3:16–18

God has done what we could never do, but in such a way that it was done by one of us. This is, perhaps, a better idea than punishing you. We now have to ask how it actually comes about in our lives, and try to discover how to avoid stopping it.

Here are some texts which further illustrate some of the ideas contained in this chapter:

> The light does not fail because of those who have blinded themselves; it remains the same, while the blinded are plunged in darkness by their own fault. Light never forces itself on anyone, nor does God use compulsion on anyone who refuses to accept his artistry.
>
> St Irenaeus, *Against the Heretics*, VI.39.3

> Jesus Christ, the Son of the living God, became our reconciliation with the Father. He it was, and he alone, who satisfied the Father's eternal love, that fatherhood that from the beginning found expression in creating the world, giving man all the riches of creation, and making him 'little less than God' (Psalm 8:6), in that he was created 'in the image and in the likeness of God' (Genesis 1:26). He and he alone also satisfied that fatherhood of God and that love which man in a way rejected ... The redemption of the world – this tremendous

mystery of love in which creation is renewed – is, at its deepest root, the fullness of justice in a human Heart – the Heart of the First-born Son – in order that it may become justice in the hearts of many human beings, predestined from eternity in the First-born Son to be children of God, and called to grace, called to love.

John Paul II, *Redemptor Hominis*, 9

In his intimate life, God 'is love', the essential love shared by the three divine Persons: personal love is the Holy Spirit as the Spirit of the Father and the Son. Therefore he 'searches even the depths of God' (1 Corinthians 2:10), as uncreated Love-Gift. It can be said that in the Holy Spirit the intimate life of the Triune God becomes totally gift, an exchange of mutual love between the divine Persons, and that through the Holy Spirit God exists in the mode of gift. It is the Holy Spirit who is the personal expression of this self-giving, of this being-love. He is Person-Love. He is Person-Gift. Here we have an inexpressible deepening of the concept of person in God, which only divine revelation makes known to us. At the same time, the Holy Spirit, being consubstantial with the Father and the Son in divinity, is love and uncreated gift from which derives as from its source all giving of gifts vis-à-vis creatures (created gift): the gift of existence to all things through creation; the gift of grace to human beings through the whole economy of salvation.

John Paul II, *Dominum et Vivificantem*, 10

By calling God 'Father', the language of faith indicates two main things: that God is the first origin of everything and transcendent authority; and that he is at the same time goodness and loving care for all his children. God's parental tenderness can also be expressed by the image of motherhood, which emphasizes God's immanence, the intimacy between Creator and creature. The language of faith thus draws on the human experience of parents, who are in a way the first representatives of God for man. But this experience also tells us that human parents are fallible and can disfigure the face of fatherhood and motherhood. We ought therefore to recall that God transcends the human distinction between the sexes. He is neither man nor woman: he is God. He also transcends human fatherhood and motherhood, although he is their origin and standard: no one is father as God is Father.

Catechism of the Catholic Church, 239

Chapter 5

THICKER THAN WATER

Then I shall give you the gift of my love.

Song of Songs 7:13

The last two chapters contained a lot of ideas and perhaps you found them rather abstract. That is a challenge with doctrines, and an important fact about them. No teaching of the Church is meant to stand alone. Each one is meant to be applied in life, each one has a bearing on our need of God and his answer to that need. If you are becoming impatient for answers to pressing questions of 'real life', please bear with me a little longer. Life will get real soon enough, and we must gather enough resources to cope with it.

It is a little surprising that the Church has not attempted to define how we are saved by Christ. You can find plenty of models and theories, but no formal definition in the same way as the Trinity or the nature of Christ is defined. Most of the doctrines we have were evolved to support the claim that we are saved in Christ. For example, the dogma of the Assumption is all about Mary as Mother of God. This ancient title was thought up to bring home the divinity of Christ in popular Marian devotion. By bearing the God-child, Mary's body was made specially holy. From earliest times, some Christians had believed that Mary was assumed into heaven (hence the marked lack of Marian relics), and Pope Pius XII chose to promulgate this officially at a time when many people were coming to wonder if Jesus was anything more than a gifted guru, a very holy man with good ideas. The special status of Mary was intended to underscore the very special status of her son.

The Assumption can seem to non-Catholics, and indeed to some Catholics, to be a bit of window-dressing: not really necessary, and a matter of taste to take or leave. But not so the claim of salvation. This is central to our faith. In fact, it *is* our faith; everything else is just corollary. Yet Christians have never been able to do more than come up with images and stories to try and describe this most important part of our religion. In some ways this is a failure, but in other ways it is quite encouraging. The reconciliation between God and human beings in Christ goes deeper than words can. It penetrates our human nature beyond sin and fall. Our doctrines are like the symptomatic description of a cold: sneezing, temperature, a tendency to be other than our usual, pleasant selves. Invisible to us is the action of the virus, and of the antibodies. The analogy breaks down because we can now describe viruses and antibodies. Perhaps it is more like trying to convey the meaning of a sentence without saying the sentence; we can never get behind words and symbols.

The earliest images and metaphors were very simple. The Cross was seen as the location of a great battle between Christ and the devil. In the resurrection we see the victory of Christ, who, like a modern marine detachment, has attacked the terrorist hideout and freed the hostages. The devil attacks Jesus, fooled by his human nature, only to be overwhelmed by the divine power concealed within. Such a way of thinking appeals to us strongly, since we naturally identify with stories. Writers such as Tolkien, Lewis and Stephen Donaldson give us the same myth in different terms. It closely relates to our own experiences of life as a struggle, sometimes with forces within us we do not understand or like very much.

The idea is sometimes more subtle. To say we are captive to the devil accords with part of our experience. But our sense of freedom and of choice leads to the idea that we also are in rebellion against God. As such, we incur the need for forgiveness so that we can escape due punishment. The debt we owe is too great for us to pay, and so God pays it in Christ taking upon himself the just deserts of our offences. It can be put more acceptably by saying that Jesus makes the sacrifice necessary to all true forgiveness. We also, however, have a sense of helpless choosing; that we know we will do the same bad thing over and over again. This is so despite all we know about God, Christ and ourselves. St Paul puts the problem in a way almost everyone can relate to from time to time:

I cannot understand my own behaviour. I fail to carry out the things I want to do, and I find myself doing the very things I hate. When I act against my own will, that means I have a self that acknowledges that the Law is good, and so the thing behaving in that way is not my self but sin living in me ... with the result that instead of doing the good things I want to do, I carry out the sinful things I do not want ... In short, it is I who with my reason serve the Law of God, and no less I who serve in my unspiritual self the law of sin.

Romans 7:14–25

Paul's predicament is that of someone who would dearly love to be able to swim the English Channel. Exercises, practices, diets cannot alter a basic inability to swim for twenty-odd miles. He just cannot do it. Nor can I, and nor can you, I would guess. Such a way of thinking leads to saying that there is something damaged about our very human nature. We know perfectly well what we are called to by God, but our daily experience can be more like that of fish trying to build a space rocket: just not what we are made for.

A more theologically respectable way of putting it would be to say that the image of God has been wiped out, or at least defaced, in us. Where we should reflect a true picture of God's love, we produce a dim and scattered chaos. It is possible, though, to get this very wrong. One can think, for example, that the spirit is willing, while the flesh is weak. This truth is taken too far if we mean that we are good spirits trapped in a body of sin. St Paul sometimes says things like this, but not in this meaning. For him, the whole human, soul and body, is fallen; not something anyone with honest insight into themselves would dispute.

If our whole nature was fallen, our whole nature is restored in Christ. This is why the Church has always insisted on the full and real humanity of Jesus. The idea is that by contact with his divine nature, the human nature was revivified and restored. Some thinkers took this further to say that we become divinized in Christ, though it is never easy to say what that means. Christ became what we are, so that we may become what he is. Pressing the idea leads us to horrible complexities about Christ's human soul, and how to square his real human knowledge with his real divine omniscience.

Fortunately we do not have to solve any of these; my money is on those fish beating us to it if we try. Each of the views outlined has its own problems and inconsistencies. The devil does not seem any less vigorous now than he was before; indeed, advancing human technology seems to give him a positive advantage. That God should slay his own Son to satisfy his just vengeance does not encourage one to approach the throne of grace. Jesus bearing the pain of our forgiveness is touching, but not always relevant if we ignore it, while his exalting of our nature seems to make our actions irrelevant. But I hope it is also clear that each of the views contains insight into our condition. For example, the satisfaction 'theory' in itself shows our reluctance to take seriously the parable of the Prodigal Son.

A problem these views have in common, perhaps, is that they are quite abstract. Undoubtedly we have a human nature, but it is not very tangible in itself. What is tangible is our collection of broken loves and fallen promises. Troops mopping up resistance after the decisive battle are just as vulnerable to individual bullets as they were before the victory. Knowing our forgiveness, we still sin. The question of what incarnation, death and resurrection have to do with us today still needs to be asked.

Part of an answer can be gained from looking at where we start. Most of us live more or less scattered lives in less or more satisfactory relations with other scattered livers. What do we miss? One vital thing is the realization of our state. I have described this state as one of need, of dissatisfaction, of incompleteness, of fear, frustration, boredom, loss, sorrow, whatever. The acknowledgement of this state I have called faith, though it so often looks like doubt. The second thing is the sense that the emptiness is not all there is, or all there might be. We still try to get on with each other, and regret the times when we do not. This sense is called hope. The last ingredient is a foundation to both, a still point against which we can rest whatever may happen. It may not surprise you if I call this love.

Imagine that you are the cook for a large group of people. They live in the middle of a desert and are very hungry. You are sorry for them and do your best to feed them. It involves spending most of the day gathering the small plants and roots that grow in the rocks, and the nights digging for water in which to soak them so they are soft enough to eat. There are just enough stringy weeds, but only just. You do your best, but it is still not what they need, let alone what they want. So relations are strained. You have come to resent their demands as much as they resent your failure to satisfy them. One night a mysterious stranger appears and puts in your hand a cardboard box full of cheese and pickle sandwiches. You are so famished you eat them all, and then the box. He comes the next night, and you wolf the lot. Now you can have sandwiches, you don't want roots and plants, and you eat the box only to hide the evidence. And so you no longer find food for other people with the same zest; you are not hungry like they are. Some time later, now you are better fed, you spare a glance for the nocturnal stranger. He has changed recently: more haggard about the eyes, thin about the wrists. This will not do! You cannot have him starving to death, worn out with fetching food; no more sandwiches if he dies. You offer him a sandwich: 'Why don't you have one?' He looks at you and answers, 'Because they are for you.' And then you understand.

It is the same with our lack of love. We cannot love as we should, as others need. We do not love ourselves even. But this is exactly where we are made in the image and likeness of God, in our ability to relate to other persons; or, more precisely, in our inability not to interact. The blessing has become a curse, as our inner loss spreads. We do not have enough for ourselves, still less for others. But then, in the middle of the fallen world a man speaks words the like of which men and women were created to speak:

> I am the bread of life. Anyone who comes to me will never be hungry; anyone who believes in me will never thirst ... Your fathers ate the manna in the desert and they are dead; but this is the bread that comes down from heaven, so that you can eat it and not die. I am the living bread that has come down from heaven. Anyone who eats this bread will live for ever; and the bread that I shall give is my flesh for the life of the world.
>
> John 6:35, 50–51

Jesus offers you love, for you, and for you to pass on. He gives what was lacking, the real food we long for from God and from each other. He stands in the middle of the human race and hands out his bread to all who will take it. Thus we can talk of the raising of our nature; there is a relating 'I' among us who loves as we should love. We can take his food, gorge on it, and then learn to imitate his sacrifice.

It is not simply a matter of example. Let us think a little about that sacrifice. The bread is not quite how we would like it; not in nice soft white slices. It is a rough and broken bread, 'my flesh for the life of the world'. The agony of the Cross is not an obvious sign of the love of God. But Christ's love is so full, and so different from ours, because it was taken even to the last resort: 'Father, forgive them, they do not know what they are doing.' We have to appreciate the depth of choice involved in the Passion of Jesus. At any point he could have answered his taunters and saved himself. At any point he could have summoned the power that stilled storms and gave sight to the blind. At any point, God could have intervened in tiny, invisible ways to prevent the situation becoming humanly inevitable.

He did not, for the same reason that he will not just punish us, or scrap the whole world and start again. Christ resisting his Cross would have been an act of self-defence, of aggression such as we do every day. He could have defended himself, with swords or thunderbolts, but at the expense of those around him. This is what makes the difference. His love consists of a total giving of himself, unmixed with anything else, any other interest, any other motive. It is the love which the Father and Son share in the Holy Spirit, the same love which overflowed in the creation of you and me and the whole world, and the same love we were meant to show to each other in him and to him in each other. But we say 'no' to God and to ourselves and to others in a thousand little ways each day. Christ fulfilled the will of God, gave to the Father a total 'yes' because at each stage he responded with the gift of love. At last, there was a part of creation which no longer held up God's grace with resistance.

All we have to do is get in touch with Christ, and keep in touch. The Church exists simply as a way of doing this, so that Christ walks with each person the path of life. In some senses, it is *the* way of doing this. Catholics believe that in the Church, God gives us the love of Christ, and a community in which to share it. The theological term for this is 'sacrament'. Before we think about sacraments, however, it is time to make concrete some of the doctrines we have looked at. We now have sufficient resources to make some sense of everyday life.

PART 2

THE LIFE WE LIVE

Chapter 6

GET REAL

But they give solidity to the created world.

Ecclesiasticus 38:34

The aim of this chapter is to show how the doctrines we have been exploring can impact on the way we see everyday life. The Gospel is about Jesus Christ, the God who lives with us. Let us begin with the part of life which is perhaps the least likely candidate for finding God: the daily drudge of working (or, worse, not working) for our living.

The modern period has witnessed a large degree of confusion about the purpose and value of work. In the ancient world, things were much simpler. Greek culture, for example, thrived on the institution of slavery, which left a large leisured class able to enjoy the delights of politics, the theatre and warfare. Such a way of organizing society was not simply convenient, it actually reflected what were perceived as fundamental facts about human beings. It was not just the case that slaves were people who had fallen on hard times, or were the captives of vanquished enemies. People became slaves because they were that type of people, understood as almost a separate species. As Aristotle put it, 'The natural slave is one qualified to be, and therefore is, the property of another or who is only so far a human being as to understand reason without himself possessing it' (*Politics*, 1.5).

It is hardly necessary to trace the path of such thinking through history. Perhaps the clearest expression is in the eighteenth-century description of those who did no work at all as 'people of quality'. Nor is it fair to blame the Greeks. Aristotle was cited only because he gives such a bald statement of what is so easily assumed. The same perceptions would have been found in ancient – Old Testament – Israel. Even in this economically very simple, agricultural society, wealth, and the consequent ability to have servants and be freed from daily drudge, was seen as a sign of righteousness and of blessing. Though the wicked may prosper for a short while, the psalmist assures us that this is done on credit, and that we shall soon see his widow and children begging in the streets. When Job is suddenly cast into utter destitution, the only explanation his comforters can find is that he must somehow have sinned without knowing it. It is but a step from saying that riches are a sign of God's favour to saying that rich people are the people that God likes. Such thinking underlies the Pharisees' statement about Jesus in St John's Gospel that 'as for this man, we do not even know where he comes from'. Which is simply a way of saying that he obviously does not come from the right place, the right people.

The market place

We have to face the fact that for most people, the word 'work' is synonymous with that of 'toil'. There are two opposing tendencies, which to some degree are present in everyone. One is to minimize work as much as possible, to adopt the attitude of one who 'clocks' on and off with little regard for what is done in between, and little sense of purpose in it. The other is to be workaholic, to be someone who cannot stop, who stays late at work or even brings it home at weekends. In some senses, work has become his, or her, life. It would be unwise to rhapsodize about the supreme Christian value of work unless it is taken on board that work is for many a kind of trap, in either futility or the hectic pursuit of rewards that the pursuer then has no time to enjoy. An example of the first is the treadmill of industrial production so well documented in Victorian social fiction, and still to be seen in the sweatshops of emerging Asian economies, while the second is a phenomenon recognizable to many a tired commuter.

What is it that lies at the root of these problems, that has made work a more deadly enemy of the soul than idleness? Perhaps it might be summed up in the word 'alienation'. The issue can be put very simply. Some people have work which is obviously fulfilling. Take doctors, for example. They spend their day either curing people or helping them to bear their suffering. At the same time they do much to support friends and relatives of the sick, and provide a genuine and real witness of love in society. Their work contributes, and they see the result. While most doctors would seek to diminish the rosy glow about their profession, it remains an example of what the Second Vatican Council had in mind when it said:

> When men and women provide for themselves and their families in such a way as to be of service to the community as well, they can rightly look upon their work as a prolongation of the work of their creator, a service to their fellow men, and their personal contribution to the fulfilment in history of the divine plan.
>
> *Gaudium et Spes*, 34

The same could easily be said of teachers, social workers and many others. But again, if we look around at the majority, it just does not seem to apply. How does a man in a production line turning out, say, sports cars, contribute to society? You might say that he provides necessary means of transport. But who buys sports cars? Not many people, and certainly not the men who make them. A rather disproportionate amount of society's resources of labour and materials thus goes towards providing a particular, and perhaps unnecessary, means of transport for rather a few people. If we raise the stakes, as *Gaudium et Spes* does in the passage just quoted, and ask how he contributes to 'the fulfilment in history of the divine plan', the answer seems either too precious for words, or else patronizing in the extreme. So, let us raise the stakes even more, by seeing how the Council continues:

> Moreover, we believe by faith that through the homage of work offered to God, man is associated with the redemptive work of Jesus Christ, whose labour with his hands at Nazareth greatly ennobled the dignity of work.
>
> *Gaudium et Spes*, 67

How can this bear on the unemployed, the inhabitants of South American shanty towns, or those trapped in prostitution? Perhaps it seems that the Church's approach to human work bears all the hallmarks of its sources in the rich capitalist minority who benefit from the whole terrible mess.

We have two levels of alienation at the same time. On the one hand, people drudge away at something whose only direct bearing on their lives is that it provides them, if they are lucky, with the means to survive and raise children trapped in the same toil. On the other hand, 'the implacable process of work for gain' can itself be dehumanizing. People who do rotten jobs, or none at all, are easily seen as inferior; and easily see themselves as inferior. What is more, the unending experience of futility in the way one spends most of one's time has its effect on one's actual being. What we do can change what we are in ourselves. Mr Gradgrind in Dickens' *Hard Times* was not created such; he made himself so. A contrast to this is the doctor or teacher, whose work can be, at the level of ideal, an expression of their being, of their desire to be and do good; in non-secular terms, to be holy. But this is not the norm, and if we accept that the norm is in general quite the opposite, then the Church seems to be well out of step in what it teaches about the value of work, as has already been seen.

There is, however, a third level of alienation, which gives some clue to a way forward. It is a curious phenomenon of social history that at some point work became something that one went out to do. We talk of domestic work and so on, but it is not seen or treated as work in the same way as, say, ploughing a field or brokering a used car deal. The 'traditional' pattern of family life, where the house-wife's task was to make life possible and comfortable to the 'bread-winner', exemplifies this division. The economic value of work in the home does not necessarily feature in national GDP figures. Should it? The trouble with the division is that we end up with a very artificial conception of what work is. It is seen as something which earns money from 'outside' or which benefits those outside the family. Work is judged then according to what it brings in, whether to the family or to society as a whole. And so is the worker. But then all those things on which we cannot put a value, the devotion of a mother, the child washing up, or the family relaxing together, are taken as having no value, which is not true at all. What this implies is that the focus on what is done and for whom is misleading.

The work of God

Our hard-won doctrines of Incarnation and Redemption offer a way forward. Who is Jesus? Where does he come from? We have just seen how easily work can become bound up with judgements about status, and indeed about whether someone is human at all. By way of contrast, St Paul, in his letter to the Philippians, gives us a hymn about one who, though in the form of God, accepted the human state and became obedient even to the shameful death of a criminal. The Word has become flesh and dwelt among us. Everything is changed by this, including our work, because

> the one who, while being God, became like us in all things, devoted most of the years of his life to manual work at the carpenter's bench. This circumstance in itself constitutes the most eloquent 'Gospel of work', showing that the basis for determining the value of work is not primarily the kind of work that is done but the fact that the one doing it is a person.
>
> Pope John Paul II, *Laborem Exercens*, 6

In other words, human activity is valuable because it is done by human beings. To get the right view of work, we have to get the right view of humanity. This statement of John Paul II turns all that has been said above on its head. Instead of thinking of particular types of work as relatively admirable (astronaut, stockbroker, pop star) and others as degraded (dustman, farmhand, politician) we should think that each is done by a human being, created and loved by God. If we really want to know what is valuable, then we should look at what Christ did. Having found him performing a simple and humble task, we have to ask more searching questions about our judgements of value.

Our talk about work contains an ambiguity. On the one hand, the first creation account in Genesis explicitly depicts God as working for six days to create the world, and implies that human work is a reflection of that divine toil. At a more mundane level, teenagers around the world are urged to find a career that will use their own particular talents and interests, in which they may hope to find some fulfilment. On the other hand, the toil of work is seen as a consequence of the Fall, as a part of the curse of Adam in the second chapter of Genesis. In an ideal world, one might not have to work – there would be plenty for everyone and it would all be for the asking. It is as a result of our sin that we have to live by the sweat of our brow. This is a universal law, under which we serve. One approach gives us the much-derided 'work ethic', while the other leaves little room for seeing value in anything we do. A corrective to such a way of thinking was given by the great nineteenth-century pope, Leo XIII, in the first of what has become a series of 'social encyclicals':

> Even had man never fallen from a state of innocence, he would not have been wholly unoccupied; but that which would have been a free choice and his delight became afterwards compulsory, and the painful expiation of his disobedience.
>
> *Rerum Novarum*, 14

Pope Leo's text acknowledges that to do things is part of our human nature and so, following the Eden story, there was work before the Fall. This fits with some of our instincts that much of what we do is, in principle, blessed and even fun. There is something intrinsically good and pleasurable about preparing a meal for a family, or working with a child to make a bird-box or paint a chair. What has gone wrong is the context, where we are too rushed to do those things properly, or too stressed by our feelings of inadequacy to take it when Tom won't eat his greens. But this holds out a hope that work, since it is not a punishment, could actually be a blessing if only other things were equal. Thinking like that may then spur us to look at our own lives or, if we have that kind of power, the lives we force others to lead in our factories and shops.

It is not our power to act and work which has resulted in today's sorry mess, but our tendency to use that power to do other things than know love and serve the God who gave it. The correct understanding of work is therefore not to be found in socio-economic analyses, but in an examination of the human condition itself.

As such, it does not appear to matter what people do, so long as they are people. This then forms the basis for a morality of work; one asks what kinds of work dehumanize. Obvious examples are forced labour in chain gangs, and surgeons who perform abortions. But what is it that is so special about human beings?

The initial answer comes from the first Genesis creation account. The seven-day pattern is designed to lead us to a climax:

the culmination of God's work is the creation of man in God's image. God is depicted as one who works, and the man or woman who works expresses this fact of their nature. From this we gain the idea that human work has a very special value. It is not philosophically necessary that humans should be active at all – we can imagine creatures, albeit rather boring ones, which show no sign of action or change. But that is not how we are made; we are human *doings* not just human *beings* – if you will pardon the phrase – because God is himself in creative action:

> The word of God's revelation is profoundly marked by the fundamental truth that man, created in the image of God, shares by his work in the activity of the Creator and that, within the limits of his own human capabilities, man in a sense continues to develop that activity, and perfects it as he advances further in the whole of creation.
>
> John Paul II, *Laborem Exercens*, 25

But God does not simply create. He also acts to save us from the consequences of our misuse of the divine power of activity which he has put within us. The key event of this work is the life, death and resurrection of Jesus Christ. It is hard to take on board the significance of the Incarnation, the doctrine that, in Christ, the second person of the Trinity has taken on our human nature. Everything that Our Lord did in his life on earth has saving value, and this includes especially the work he did.

Usually, one tends to see this as an example of humility and of humble service. Jesus slaving away at the carpenter's bench can encourage us to plod on with our own column of figures or heap of bricks. However, the fact that it was *God* who was doing it changes everything. It takes us beyond the merely exemplary. 'Jesus not only proclaimed but *first and foremost fulfilled by His deeds* the "Gospel", the word of Wisdom that had been entrusted to Him' (John Paul II, *Laborem Exercens*, 26; emphasis added). The fulfilment of the words of the Gospel is our salvation; that is what the Gospel is 'good news' about. Jesus working in Nazareth redeems our lives, because he redeems our work; that apparently pointless drudge is given eternal value because God bothered to do it. What is more, whatever humans do in their God-given capacity for action can be grace bearing, since it is done by human persons restored to the full image of God who took on himself their nature.

Real life

Perhaps this seems too grand a vision of the daily round of the office or the factory. But we must bear in mind who is doing that daily grind; it is a human person in the image of God. It is this which gives it its value in God's eyes, which is the only real value. But what about the problems of alienation mentioned above? Am I not in danger of expounding a utopian picture of fulfilling work against a background of deep suffering and experienced futility? After all, Marx pointed out how religion can function as the opiate of the masses, insulating them from present sufferings by reference to a better world. One can go on for ever about the glory of God in man, and still leave untouched the real human situation of misery and sin. It is necessary to make these high doctrines of creation and redemption touch our lives at the points of suffering. The foundation has already been laid, in Pope Leo's talk of expiation. Building on this, John Paul II makes the point fully explicit:

> The Christian finds in human work a small part of the Cross of Christ and accepts it in the same spirit of redemption in which Christ accepted his Cross for us ... On the one hand, this confirms the indispensability of the Cross in the spirituality of human work; on the other hand, the Cross which this toil constitutes reveals a new good springing from work itself, from work understood in depth and in all its aspects and never apart from work.
>
> *Laborem Exercens*, 27

To know what an authentically human life looks like, we have to look at Christ. The incarnation of the Son of God ended in the agony of Calvary. This is the central mystery of our redemption, that it comes through suffering and death. Just as significant as the life of God in Christ is the death of God in Christ. We have therefore to set against the apparently over-glossy picture of work as participation in God's creative power the starker vision of work as part of the sufferings of the Body of Christ. It is this that we find reflected in the barren nature of so much social life and exchange. The whole creation is, as St Paul said, subjected to futility in Christ.

The difference for a Christian worker is that he can accept his burden in the same spirit as Christ did. That spirit was one of saving love, and also of such faith in God that the issue of the death was resurrection. This is what the Pope means by his reference to the 'new good springing from work itself'. Sooner or later we have to confront the fact that Christians are meant to transform the society in which they live as yeast does the bread, and that this is done by participation in its woes, but by participation also in faith and in hope. A while ago, I hinted at a definition of work as that which we are reluctant to do. If we make this as broad as possible, it includes the unwelcome idleness of unemployment or destitution; unpleasant and unacceptable realities which God has accepted into himself on the Cross.

To imagine that the only holy things are the nice things that seem religious – church services, people doing good, prayer, beautiful music and pictures, and especially work that manifestly fulfils the worker and benefits everyone else – is not simply to evacuate most of what we actually do of meaning and significance. It is to misunderstand the implications of the Incarnation. God is present in ordinary secular realities because God lived those realities in Jesus as much as you or I live them today. But this means that they are holy and full of power to create and save. The conviction that God is not really found in those things that bore or hurt us prevents us accepting those burdens in the redeeming spirit of Christ. But it goes further than that. Suppose we widen the definition of work from being simply economically productive activity. The more general idea is of any human action, be it designing planes or washing dishes or brushing one's teeth or combing a child's hair. Each of these is an action by a human person, and as such each is holy, because each is in fact the work of God.

We matter to him that much. If he has lived our real lives, so can we in him. It is time to see how this can be done each day for everyone we know.

Chapter 7

THE MISSING LINK

Listen to me, faint hearts, who feel far from victory.

Isaiah 47:12

One of the many delights of my novitiate in the monastery was Christmas. The great thing was that novices were only allowed to send twelve Christmas cards. This was a liberation; no need to try and remember who sent one to me last year, no searching through drawers for lost change-of-address cards, and no worries about forgetting a vital aunt or cousin, since I could say to myself that I had not had enough cards to send. There was a slight edge of guilt to the liberation, however, because I received lots of cards, the usual number, plus a few from people who thought they would never see me again now I was a monk. It is amazing how much a Christmas card can mean. There are some people with whom one has no contact at all apart from a scribbled 'must meet up soon' note on the back of the envelope, but who are yet still 'in touch' and ready to pick up the threads of a friendship where they were last left.

If you have ever felt a small lift at getting a card or letter from a relative or acquaintance you had not thought about for years, or else a slight 'humph' when someone forgets your birthday or wedding anniversary, then you already intuitively understand what sacraments are about. The definition in the old English Penny Catechism which people used to learn off by heart said that 'a sacrament is an outward sign of inward grace, ordained by Jesus Christ, by which grace is given to our souls' (n. 249). In less theological language, this means that a sacrament is a way of getting in touch with Christ, and keeping in touch. Just as a Christmas card is an expression and confirmation of a relationship with someone far away, so a sacrament expresses to us the love of Christ. It also gives us, contains, the love of Jesus, just as a card can in some ways be the friendship, if it is our only contact with the other person.

Of course, we have other contacts: memories, mutual friends, past gifts and the hope of meeting again. In the same way we have lots of contact with God: the creation, our neighbour, the Bible and so on. A sacrament is a special contact, however, since it is a way of meeting his eye. To push the comparison further, a sacrament is like meeting the love of your life. Anything else is just postcards, photos and dreams. St John of the Cross puts the idea quite beautifully in a poem about The Soul and the Bridegroom, speaking to Jesus:

> Show me your face, my Lover,
> even though beauty seen unveiled should kill,
> let it be so! Discover
> your presence, if you will,
> at once the cause and cure of all my ill.
>
> O crystal spring clear-shining,
> if on your silver surface could appear
> those eyes for which I'm pining –
> suddenly and quite near! –
> whose image printed deep within I bear ...
>
> ... You looked with love on me,
> and deep within, your eyes imprinted grace;
> this mercy set me free,
> held in your love's embrace,
> to lift my eyes, adoring, to your face.

> *The Soul and the Bridegroom,*
> translated by Marjorie Flower OCD

He means it

Some people have difficulty when such erotic language is used to express the relation we are offered with God. This is, however, the very point behind sacraments. Jesus wants to touch our everyday lives, not in order to take us out of the nasty material world, but in order to redeem that nasty material world which his Father made and said was good, and to live in it with us, through us. A sacrament is therefore a physical sign, because it is the whole person, body and soul, who is loved and redeemed in it. So, for baptism we have water; for confirmation, oil; for eucharist, food; for reconciliation, words of forgiveness; for ordination and the sick or dying, anointing; for matrimony, vows and sexual union.

Let us recall for a moment what is at stake. We live in a wrecked way, our God-like ability to relate to each other and ourselves scattered into mixed loves and selfish wants, along with yearning for good and truth. In Jesus, we are offered a relationship which, from one end, is different. It is real love, pure self-gift. Relating to him, our ability to love becomes schooled and healed. Relating to others, in him, we can pass on the gift and so play our part in slowly healing others. Sacraments are the missing link between us and Christ, the meeting place with the one true Lover.

Perhaps the clearest case of this is in Christian marriage. Time and again in the Old Testament, the relation of God to his people is pictured as one of total union, complete devotion by God to a wayward, not to say unfaithful, bride. By the vows and commitment of matrimony,

> The spouses participate in it as spouses, together, as a couple, so that the first and immediate effect of marriage is ... a typically Christian communion of two persons because it represents the mystery of Christ's incarnation and the mystery of his covenant. The content of participation in Christ's life is also specific: conjugal love involves a totality, in which all the elements of the person enter – appeal of the body and instinct, power of feeling and affectivity, aspiration of the spirit and of will. It aims at a deeply personal unity, the unity that, beyond union in one flesh, leads to forming one heart and soul.
>
> John Paul II, *Familiaris Consortio*, 13

What a good and successful marriage can do for the partners and children is exactly what Christ offers to do for human society in the sacraments. The marriage is not, however, just a symbol, a typical example. It actually *is* the love of God in the world in a particular and powerful form. How powerful is shown when parents share in the creative work of God in giving life to children and nurturing them. Notice also that the Pope says that marriage involves the whole person; spirits and hearts, indeed, but also bodies and carnal desire. Sexual love and the appetite for it can be, and in a Christian marriage are, a sign of the union of Christ with the believers in the sacrament and also, for the couple and their family, that union made real, everyday, material.

This expresses the purpose of the sacramental life of the Church, to bring all parts of life into contact with Christ and his self-giving on the Cross. Perhaps some emphasis should be put on the fact that God wants contact with all parts of our life. This cannot be put too strongly, or thought about too often. The fundamental misunderstanding in our knowledge of good and evil is that our sins make us unacceptable to God. Because we know what is right and wrong, or at least that there is such a thing as right and wrong, we have acquired the ability to judge. It imprisons us and makes us miserable, because we know we have crimes on our hands. We think that God does indeed hate the sin, but do not grasp the far bigger fact that he loves the sinner. By an unfortunate chain of associations we have also learnt the idea that the bits of us connected with sins are also thereby bad, or at least suspect. Desires lead us to sin, so we suspect the normal human tendency to want things; bodies are quite useful for sinning with, so bodies have to be hidden modestly from physical and spiritual gaze. Much of the human race is stuck in a state of denial about large parts of our nature.

It should be clear by now that it is these parts that interest God most, that he most wants us to bring to him. Our tendency is to think we have to put on the right virtues and talk the right language (Latin, perhaps?) before he will hear us. But he does not want you to be good or holy; he wants you. He wants, most of all, your sins so that he can forgive them. No other offering, be it millions or dimes, is as welcome. The only things that are unacceptable to God are the things we will not offer him.

This is why he has given us the sacrament of Reconciliation or Penance, and also why we find it so hard to understand and to take advantage of confession. (We'll talk more about confession in chapter 9.) It is a frightening thing, since we might be rejected. The priest may shout at us, or laugh, or tell us we are lost. In any case it is asking too much for us to tell another, equally horrible, human being all our embarrassing secrets. We have aural confession not because the priest needs to hear our sins, or because God needs to be told about them, or because there is any virtue in public self-flagellation. We have aural confession because we need to say, and need to admit to ourselves, what we are like. Otherwise, we just prefer to pretend we do not need the help of God; a pretence that is rather deadly for you and for all.

You are a small child in a garden, playing some lonely game. Over the fence you hear the laughter of children next door, a party in progress. The smell of freshly baked cakes is in the air. You sneak round the gate and, seeing that everyone is distracted, seize some of the cakes from the ledge where they are cooling. You eat them, and stolen pleasure tastes sweet. Next week the same happens, and the same the next. A curious change comes upon you; it is now almost a compulsive grabbing of cakes. You come to resent the happy children even more fiercely, determined to deprive them. And then you are invited to the party the next week; a kind note explains that you were always welcome, but they did not realize you were too shy to come without invitation, they had, in fact, made extra cakes in case you turned up and they hope you enjoyed them, don't mention it. But how can you go, since you have already abused the hospitality? They do not need your apology, you do.

In the same way, God needs us to confess to him, because only then can he begin to heal at the deepest levels. Remember that he will not force. The question, of course, is 'Why can't I be forgiven anyway? Suppose I do admit to myself all those things, and say them to myself; why does it need the Church and a ritual?' This problem bears on all the sacraments. If God offers salvation to all, conditional only on them accepting it, why insist on this particular way?

Sacraments are guarantees, not exclusions. This is often misunderstood. You could meet your dearest friend at any time. An arrangement stands to meet for lunch next Friday. It is quite possible you will bump into each other before then, and quite right to hope that you will. But you know you will see each other on Friday at lunchtime. Similarly, sacraments are, to use the traditional phrase, 'ordained by Christ' in the sense that he promises to be there when we come to him in them. What is more, meeting in the flesh is so much more full as an expression and embodiment of friendship than, say, talking on the phone or playing answering-machine tennis.

Meeting for supper

This brings us to what is really on offer in the seven sacraments; it is put most richly in the Eucharist, the communion sacrifice of the Mass established, so far as anything can be proved, explicitly by Jesus.

> He always loved those who were his own in the world. When the time came for him to be glorified by you, his heavenly Father, he showed the depth of his love.
>
> *Roman Missal*, Eucharistic Prayer IV

Understanding of the Mass can be hindered as well as helped by our traditional language. What happens is fairly clear. We listen to God's Word to understand his message of salvation. We offer gifts of bread and wine which are changed into the Body and Blood of Christ. We then receive them in communion with the whole Church and with each other. Now try and make that convincing. For Catholics insist that the bread and wine are not just symbols of Christ's presence, they actually *are* his presence, Body and Blood, under the appearance of bread and wine. Such an insistence defies both reason and the evidence of our senses; a large technical vocabulary of 'substance', 'accidents' and 'transubstantiation' has had to be developed simply to express clearly what we are trying to mean. The idea of transubstantiation is that the bread and wine retain the appearance of bread and wine, while changing in substance to the Body and Blood of Christ. It builds on the everyday observation that things are not always what they seem, to draw a distinction between what a thing is, and what it looks like. Even if this is not very convincing as an explanation, it is at least not wrong; we want to insist on the total and real presence of Christ in the Eucharist.

Transubstantiation is a complicated doctrine, but like all other doctrines, complicated or otherwise, it is encapsulating in words a very simple truth. The truth is the unlimited gift that God makes of himself to us in Christ. How can we talk of this without reducing its significance; what words can express the depth of that love? We were given words by Jesus, and use them in each of the Eucharistic Prayers:

Take this, all of you and eat it: this is my body which will be given up
for you ... Take this, all of you and drink from it; this is the cup of my
blood, the blood of the new and everlasting covenant. It will be shed
for you and for all so that sins may be forgiven. Do this in memory of
me.

There are lots of ways in which you can give yourself to someone
else, and Jesus could have used these instead of disturbing canni-
balistic language. You can give presents and gifts, be around when
needed, be around when not needed, be around when not wanted,
keep away and respect distance, get physical, send flowers, and
even die for someone else. But what would be the need and the
friend that would inspire you to give them yourself as food?
Leaving aside madness and perversion, you would have to love
someone very much and they would have to really need it. Both
those conditions are satisfied, in God's eyes, by his relation to you.
No normal person likes talking in this way, but the fact remains that
the only way to talk about the depth to which Christ gives us himself which does not take away from that depth is to say we eat his
flesh and drink his blood.

Most of the time, perhaps, our thinking is more anaemic. We
remain comfortable with spiritualized conceptions of God's action
and symbolic language about the Eucharist. The gory language
challenges us again at a weak spot; flesh and blood is physical,
material, real. Once again, God's love is material because our life
is material, and God's love is real; more real than we are. Here
we have the point of the sacraments of initiation, of which the
Eucharist is one. The others are baptism and confirmation.

God's plunge

Baptism itself can seem very unreal indeed. We wash a baby's head.
It cries. We give it candles and things, and then go on to lunch and
the usual delights of family get-togethers. In the first few centuries
of the Church's life, the rites of initiation were rather more mysterious and terrifying than they are today, and deliberately so. For the
essence of baptism is indeed a frightening thought.

When we were baptized in Christ Jesus we were baptized in his
death; in other words, when we were baptized we went into the tomb

with him and joined him in death, so that as Christ was raised from
the dead by the Father's glory, we too might live a new life. If in union
with Christ we have imitated his death, we shall also imitate him in his
resurrection.

Romans 6:3–5

For the early Church, descent into the font for baptism was a symbol of death. Three times they were immersed, with the water
closing over their heads, before they emerged, fully initiated. St
Paul sees this as the link between Christ and ourselves; it is baptism
which sets in motion the whole life of meeting Christ and passing
him by on the other side. Baptism unites us with Jesus at his most
desperate moment, on the Cross, forsaken by God. Because Jesus
is God, forsaken, he is united with us at our every moment – when,
no matter how empty of God, we are full of need for him. The
sacrament begins something which is continued through life and in
the other sacraments; you cannot be unbaptized. Of course, you
can refuse the grace, in which case it is of no avail. As infant baptism became more common, the Western Church divided off confirmation as a separate sacrament. This gives the child when older
an opportunity to express their own personal acceptance of God's
forgiveness.

In the traditional language, baptism frees us from the stain of original sin, transmitted down the generations of humankind. Another
way to put this is that for someone who is baptized, there is always
another choice, another possibility than sin. There is the life of Christ
in us, freely offered. We can have a normal, healthy relationship with
another human being, Jesus Christ. From that can, and do, come
many more such relationships. In this way is the world made anew.

But our feet should be on the ground. Nothing happens, or so it
seems. God cannot change a child or an adult in a flash any more
than he can change the world overnight; the only way to do so
would be to destroy it and make another one. He has made you
because that was what he wanted; to write the world off and make
a better one defeats that intention. We rub things out and start
again; God saves, redeems, brings us back. Maybe our response is
more efficient and sensible, but God's is more loving.

Sacraments are not about us being lifted to God, they are about
him coming down to us in Christ, sharing every up and down with
us. The world is once again charged with his glory. Christianity is

not a religion of consolation; we accept the reality of evil and sin. But we also accept another reality, which is Christ among us. What does this mean, day to day? A hint is given in the prayer said immediately after baptism. The newly baptized is anointed with chrism (an oil), and the minister says:

> God the Father of our Lord Jesus Christ has freed you from sin, given you a new birth by water and the Holy Spirit, and welcomed you into his holy people. He now anoints you with the chrism of salvation. As Christ was anointed Priest, Prophet and King, so may you live always as a member of his body, sharing everlasting life. Amen.
>
> Rite of Baptism

'Anoint' is a very loaded word. The Hebrew for someone who has been anointed is 'Messiah', and the Greek word is 'Christ'. The Father is not messing about here. He has just anointed you as his Christ; he has made the new name literally *Christian*. It takes a whole lifetime to work out what that means; it takes a whole lifetime for us to spell out in words and actions the name God has just given. For this reason, we speak of the company of believers as the Body of Christ. You and I, by virtue of baptism, are the representatives of Christ in the world. There is more to it than that. You and I, by virtue of our baptism, *are* Christ in the world. If they do not see him in us, they will not see him.

What do we show, though? Is our life a witness of radiating sanctity, transforming all around us? Probably not. Nor, realistically, will it ever be so. There is so much that should be different if we were to be the image of God, the sacrament (the sign and the real presence) of Christ in and to the world. Most people at some time in their lives wish they were someone else. But God made you to be you. He has his eye on you constantly, and it is an eye of love.

It goes further than this. 'He made us, we belong to him' (Psalm 100:3). We are not very used to the idea that we might belong to someone; it sounds like the evil of slavery. But it is not so. A slave owner owns only the slave's time, labour and external life. The rest remains free. God made all of each of us; it is all his. But he made us not as slaves, but as free beings to be loved by him, and to love him in return. He made us each for a reason, just as we acquire belongings for a reason. Sometimes, we are like ornaments or garden gnomes, made just to be looked at and loved.

In response to what we mutant killer gnomes have made of the garden, Jesus offers another truth: 'I am the Way; I am Truth; I am Life' (John 14:6). Life is what we desire, truth is the right manner of seeing our lives and God's involvement in them. What is the Way? 'No-one can come to the Father except through me.' Christ is the only way to our goal, the only source of true comfort, the only perspective on to our lives. We come to the Father by following him.

And where did he go, so as to take us with him? The words just quoted come from Jesus' last words to his disciples before his arrest, torture and ghastly death on a cross. That is where we follow him. If our religion is about making things nice, or putting up with things that go wrong and hurt us, then our eyes are not yet opened, our ears are not yet unstopped. Our suffering, taken in the Spirit of the truth of God's love for us, is our way of following Christ to the Father. He did not suffer so that we might not suffer, but so that our suffering should be his, and so should lead us to God.

I have said nothing that we have never heard before. Why believe it? Or why dwell on it so intensely? Most of the time we are fairly agnostic about God. We think of him when things go wrong and expect him to put them right for us. Or we evade the darker questions of our being by asking all those easy, impossible questions about why God who is so good should allow suffering, disease and dictators. We stop at these doubts, not realizing that they are themselves the outpouring of the love of God within us, outraged at the wreck of his wonderful world.

But Christ does not offer us a set of answers or a set of cures. He offers us a way of living real human lives in the real world. The claim of faith is that life in Christ is different, not because it is nicer, but because it takes us, and those around us, to the God who made us and loves us. It is very simple, and it is very difficult. To really live according to the Gospel, which means simply to live as though there is a God who loves you, takes some courage; and it takes a way of looking at the world and what happens to you that is often contrary to all evidence.

But just suppose it is true. On this is based all that is truly Catholic. In the words of our profession at baptism, renewed each year at Easter, *this* is our faith. This is the faith of the Church. We are proud to profess it, in Christ Jesus our Lord. Amen.

Chapter 8

HOW TO BE BAD AT PRAYER

Let your hearts be broken, not your garments torn.

Joel 2:12

In the summer of 1999, I was ordained priest in my monastery at Ampleforth. It was, of course, a very enjoyable day, all the more so because it had been delayed for some time by illness. I had little doubt that the ordination had effected a change in me, that I was no longer quite the same. In particular, the words of the Eucharistic Prayers, so familiar, acquired a new meaning and depth. Cardinal Hume used to speak of the astonishing fact that the words of consecration are in the first person singular: 'this is *my* Body'; that the priest speaks fully in the name and person of Jesus. It is a heady thought, and the weeks after ordination were rich with its significance.

But. After a while I realized something else, something very disturbing, and was plunged into doubt and gloom. It is still sometimes true, and I admit it to you only with some difficulty and pain. You see, I did not like saying Mass. The whole experience was fundamentally unpleasant. I had to force myself to go through the whole thing and not break off. In particular, I did not believe a word of it, none of this transubstantiation gobbledegook, and none of the rest of it, the Incarnation, the love of God, and even his existence. To celebrate the liturgy with a group of the faithful seemed a dishonest fraud. I should not have been doing it.

That is rather a shocking thing for a new priest to think, let alone say. It shocked me too, to the core. I share it with you now because I realized one day what it was all about, what it meant. All those things in the paragraph above are true about me. There is a basic resistance to the grace of God in me, that makes me want to give it all up. My mistake was to think that this was at all unusual, that it was a new 'disease', that it was wrong, and that it kept me from prayer and the love of Christ. The experience, and the mistake, are common human experience.

That is just as well, for this experience is the experience of prayer. There is far too much written about prayer and spoken about prayer today. I hesitate to add to it. To pray is very easy; the things we find difficult about prayer have nothing to do with prayer. They are facts about us. To explain this, a passage from St Paul is rather helpful.

> We must hope to be saved since we are not saved yet – it is some-thing we must wait for with patience. The Spirit comes to help us in our weakness. For when we cannot choose words in order to pray properly, the Spirit himself expresses our plea in a way that could never be put into words, and God who knows everything in our hearts knows perfectly well what he means, and that the pleas of the saints expressed by the Spirit are according to the mind of God.
>
> Romans 8:25–7

We do not lack ideals of prayer. There are many kinds of these, from the old lady who stops off to pray the Rosary every day on her way home from the shops, to the young man with long fair locks of hair who seems to inhabit a different plane of meditative contemplation. Your experience may be different. Indeed, I hope it is, for then there is hope. The key phrase to bear in mind is this: 'we are not saved yet'. We are indeed on the way to God, but not there; travelling, but not arrived. If you feel that is not true about you, that you are already home and dry, then go ahead and walk on the water.

Meanwhile

If we are only on the way, what experience of God in prayer should we expect? Surely the experience of sinners. The first thing we should find in prayer is our own state, fallen. We should, if we live in the truth, feel reluctant, bored, disinclined, and anxious about whether we are doing the right thing. Only this way can we receive the grace of God's forgiving love. But this may not be an *experience* of peace and joy. Sometimes it is, but often we are left feeling dissatisfied. It is natural for human beings to feel far from God, because we are indeed far from God. Any techniques to find inner peace and calm, a sense of integrity or joy, are very useful on all sorts of levels in helping us cope with our basic disinclination for God and the pain which comes with it. But they are not prayer.

If we are honest, many of our difficulties with prayer are centred on ourselves. 'It is boring' means 'I am bored'. 'There is no point praying for the impossible' means 'I don't see any point in praying'. It is, of course, also rather tedious, and sometimes just as seemingly pointless, to put up with loved ones and children, and to eat breakfast, again and again, day after day. We do all those things, complaining, but we do them. There are incentives, or just simply the feeling of being stuck with it.

If you find you do not want to pray, or do not see the point, have a look about the world. There is a lot to be done. We have a lot to reproach God for in his care of us and of our fellow humans: charges of neglect, perverse infliction of suffering and ham-fisted interventions. What do *you* do? Most of us try and give a bit of cash to good causes, and even governments are starting to offer tax breaks for gifts to charity. Money is all very well, but it is only money. What about God's action? It is indeed very deficient, and if he were the director of a charity we would sack him. But why is it deficient? Aid charities find that fundraising is the easiest part of their job. The really difficult task is to get the funds to those who need it. There is also a vast fund of divine love waiting to be unleashed by just a little bit of human consent. Why not supply it by praying for those who need so much that we already have? If corrupt dictators hold up funds and use them to buy missiles, hostile humans, like you and I, divert grace to our selfish ends: help *me* pray, make *me* holy. And because it is selfish, it is our power and not God's.

For this reason it is worse than useless demanding that we should be sincere in our prayer. It is *our* prayer, and we are not sincere creatures; we are not saved yet. Even fairly benign requests like 'give us this day our daily bread' are filled with greed, with envy, and with fear that they will not be answered. Even the most exemplary attitude of dependence on the gifts of God, of awareness of his presence, is valueless unless we remember with all our hearts those who are deprived of the necessities of life, without which the likes of you and I would not have the faith to pray. For most people there is famine of one kind or another. Unless we have the courage to confront and accept the famine within ourselves, we are not living by the truth, and our prayer is not prayer, but self-assurance.

If, therefore, you think you are no good at praying, and will even admit that you do not pray regularly or even at all, then you are a very promising candidate for the highest reaches of mystical contemplation. The reason is that you understand a basic truth, which is that we do not, at some deeper and important levels of our being, want God, his love, his salvation or anything he might choose to give. It is the force of this truth that I felt, once the euphoria of ordination had worn off a bit. For this reason I offer you my experience of hating prayer, because it is an experience common to us all, if we are honest.

More than this, it is the experience that Jesus himself has shared with us. The Cross stands as an obvious low point in his relationship with God. It is also depicted in the Gospels as a moment of supreme triumph. The desolate and forsaken man is able to exclaim, 'It is accomplished,' and commit his life into the hands of God. The crucifixion makes sense as a credible human experience only as the outcome of a life of fidelity to the love of the Father. The anonymous writer of the New Testament letter to the Hebrews describes the prayer of the Son of God like this:

> During his life on earth he offered up prayer and entreaty, aloud and in silent tears, to the one who had the power to save him out of death, and he submitted so humbly that his prayer was heard.
>
> Hebrews 5:7–8

Here is no vision of serenity, or of effortless calm and peace, or of sentimental piety, but of striving and the agony of true compassion. Jesus, in prayer, experienced some of the trauma and difficulty that you might recognize from your own experiences of trying to pray. He seems to have encountered problems and the kinds of frustrations that lead to tears. Of course, for him it may well have been an overflow of love and compassion, whereas for us it tends to be selfishness and reluctance. But because Jesus' prayer was as human as ours, we have the opportunity to be as good at prayer as him, who came to share the consequences of our rejection of what is good. The difference is that he moved beyond it. The letter continues that

Son though he was, he learned to obey through suffering; but having
been made perfect, he became for all who obey him the source of
eternal salvation.

Hebrews 5:9–10

Christ became like us in all things but sin. He offered the trials and
infidelity of human beings to the Father, on the Cross, but also in
each human breath. As a result, his prayer was heard. So can ours
be.

The sign and seal of this is his resurrection. From time to time,
people like to wonder whether this happened, and whether it would
matter if we one day discovered the bones of Jesus. Of course it
would. The Resurrection is the central fact and mystery of the
Christian faith. Without it, all we have is comforts and good intentions. With it, we have the real possibility that in Jesus, God will
raise up our dead actions and make them his own in glory. The
Resurrection is what happens to people who will submit to God
with their whole being. 'Submit', of course, means to accept his
love, and to live with it and by it. It is not, and never is, an esoteric
spiritual event, in which we get absorbed into some kind of world
soul or universal consciousness. It is the resurrection of the body,
of the whole fallen and dead human being, into the glory of
redeemed *flesh*. Our daily prayer can be a part of the death and
dying. If it feels dusty, dry and lifeless, this is a good sign that God
is raising it up in ways we may not know until truly all is accomplished and we commend our spirit into the Father's hands.

So what do we do?

Perhaps the second most common reason for being put off prayer
(though it might come in third place after the disedifying behaviour
of some people who do seem to pray a lot) is that one does not
know what to do. Should I say some prayers, out of a book, or out
of my heart? Should I just sit silent, in which case what about distractions? Should I really take time out of family to be 'still' before
the Lord? Should I be repentant, or happy, reverent, or familiar?
Should I be in a church, at home, or on a street corner? Can I drink
coffee while I pray, or smoke?

This is all a bit absurd, though very hard to avoid in practice, like
many of our absurdities. Suppose you are in a room, alone, and

waiting for a very important interview. The person in the office on the other side of the door is going to submit you to a very searching series of questions, on which your whole future depends. You run a hand through your hair, and then check it is not disarranged. The dirt under your fingernails becomes luminously obvious, and you scratch away at an old stain on your cuff. You hold up your head, practising bright, positive, assertive confidence; and then hang it, to try submissive, humble acquiescence. You try out some opening lines, harumph your throat a few times, hitch up the trousers or straighten the skirt.

Then, making you jump, your name is called. It is time for the interview. As you head for the door, you realize that the voice came from inside the waiting room. The person who should be safely behind an oak door was right next to you all the time, watching your pantomime of preparation. You smile nervously, raising insouciant eyebrows. Until you realize you are wearing odd shoes.

We would laugh at such an experience of others, and have repetitive nightmares of something similar happening to us. Yet the same ridiculous act goes into prayer, or attempts to pray: finding the right words, putting yourself into the right state of mind (reverent, fearful, full of faith, contrite, righteous, whatever), being acceptable, hiding thoughts and feelings that do not seem terribly religious really, and so on. We imagine that God cannot see, does not know, until we start praying. But of course he does, he is there all the time. We imagine we can clean ourselves up so as not to appear quite so repulsive to him, so as not to feel so awkward under the gaze of unfathomable integrity.

We cannot, of course. The Father does not want us to either. He wants us to be real, to tell him the truth; he knows it anyway. He wants our trust, wants us to be willing, almost happy, to be totally embarrassed in his presence. For only then will we understand his love and mercy, and thank him with praise and glory. This is not to advocate familiarity. Such can be as false, and much more forced, than cringing and last-minute attempts to clean up. But we should do God the credit of treating him as a person.

And what kind of person? In fact, the only person with whom we can have an open and honest relationship in total safety and without fear of rejection or abuse. The thing to do in prayer, therefore, is whatever comes naturally, and whatever is authentic to you at this moment. Tell God about it, about your day, the people who have annoyed you, the people you have annoyed, and those who have helped or been helped. Give over joys and frustrations as they occur to you. As distractions occur, pray for them, especially if they are angry or shaming thoughts (it is quite common to have the most bizarre stray daydreams when trying to pray). But never seek calm, quiet detachment, unless it is given to you. The model of prayer is the Cross, sharing with God the needs of the world and his frustration when his grace is blocked off from meeting them.

Distractions can be very useful. A woman once said to me that she could not pray because she lived too close to Heathrow airport, that the noise of the planes was too much. It hardly needs pointing out that each person on every plane was in urgent need of prayer! Often, the things which disturb us when we are trying to pray are the very things to pray for, because they tend to be the things that concern us at the moment. The trick to prayer is not to clear your mind, but to offer everything that is in it to God. Perhaps there are the children to look after. Loving care of other human beings can never truly be a distraction from God, if we just remember that he is there with us. If you are cooking a meal for a friend or partner, you cannot be with them in the living room when things in the kitchen require attention. But you are doing it for them, so in a sense you are with them. On the other hand, if you spend all your time cooking, and none talking, you don't get very far in a friendship. Many couples could testify to the way in which we use activity to avoid facing each other. But as in a marriage, so in prayer, we need to spend a bit of time together. There is nothing to stop you inviting your friend into the kitchen while you cook, and no reason why Christ would not accept such an invitation.

There are two ways of praying that especially delight God, because of their transparency and trust. One is to say that you don't want to pray at the moment, can't be bothered, really, and are off to do something with more point, like watch paint dry. If you can add a wish that things were otherwise, but there it is, then you have prayed as perfectly as anyone can in your position. The Father can use that kind of honesty, and will surprise you with the gift of conscious prayer at the most unexpected and sometimes inconvenient moments.

The other kind of prayer that I think goes down very well is to tell God exactly what you think of him. Maybe you are angry at something that has happened to you, or to someone you love, or just at the unfairness and injustice of human life. It is better to have it out than to hide it in insincere piety. In the last chapter, I suggested, as a throwaway line, that people who refuse to believe in God because of all the pain and suffering in the world may indeed have a deep faith and a divine compassion, sharing God's own frustration.

Only by being true to ourselves before God can we offer our lives to him for healing and resurrection. Only by offering your life can you begin to change those around you, and those further away. In particular, only by offering the things about ourselves that we do not want to think about – sin, the raw reality of our deeper, uncontrolled rejections of Christ – can we allow God to do what he most wants, which is to heal and bless. That is the reality of Christian prayer, the faith that moves mountains.

Chapter 9

SHADOW BOXING

Stop being watchful and anxious, for I am your God.

Isaiah 41:10

All Catholics are baptized, and most are eventually confirmed. Nearly all have been to Mass at some time and received communion. Most get married, and some of those who do not are ordained instead (or as well, if you are a permanent deacon). The sacrament of the sick has instinctive appeal, especially at the point of death. But hardly anyone goes to confession.

Why not? In some ways this might seem the most appealing sacrament. For the price of a few minutes' difficult facing up to issues, the whole slate can be wiped clean; whatever was on your conscience from however long ago is taken from you by Christ. Listen to the words by which he does it, from the Prayer of Absolution:

> God the Father of mercies, through the death and resurrection of Jesus Christ his Son, has reconciled the world to himself and sent the Holy Spirit among us for the forgiveness of sins. Through the ministry of his Church, may God grant you pardon and peace, and I absolve you of your sins in the name of the Father and of the Son and of the Holy Spirit. Amen.

If anything sums up the pain and confusion of our life, and its greatest hopes, it is those words, 'pardon and peace'. This is what we all desire somewhere. It is what we strive for, even in our sins. Here it is for you now. So why do we all turn away?

The most obvious candidate for blame is the way the Church has packaged the sacrament. If you hand someone a large parcel, beautifully wrapped and fragrant, they tend to open it without much hesitation, especially if you say, 'It's for you.' If you hand someone a parcel done up in dull brown paper, half-stuck with tape, they will probably open it. But if you take the same parcel, torn at the edges and covered with mud, and present it with a scowl, they are not so likely to tear it open with squeals of delight. That is what traditional confession in a confessional box can look like. To be honest, that is what it looks like to me; you would not get me there with wild horses or even a crane.

What's wrong?

Maybe there is nothing wrong with the old ways in themselves. The point is simply that they are rather unattractive unless you have spent years getting used to them, and sometimes even then. This is especially the case if custom or upbringing trapped one into an obligatory weekly ritual which gradually became automatic and lost any meaning it once had. Associations of confession with punishment and humiliation (self-inflicted or otherwise) could be reinforced by over-enthusiastic catechesis of children, or even of adults. But it should be clear that there is nothing in modern Catholics hostile to the idea of Reconciliation in itself. This is important because the problems we have with Confession do not come from a lack of a sense of sin; though some think they do. You can buy books called *Whatever Happened to Sin?* The book I have with that title is actually a very good book about moral theology. But its title plays on the thought that we have no idea of wrongdoing, that everything has gone all lovey-dovey, and Catholics have gone soft.

Better, though, to have a soft heart than a hard one. A very frequent reason why people do not go to confession is a particular priest, a bad experience, often in childhood. Men and women have been driven away by harsh and hostile judgements flung at them without understanding by God's ministers. Everyone makes mistakes from time to time, mishears or misjudges a difficult situation. But a priest in confession, speaking in the person of Christ himself, is in a uniquely powerful position to do harm. It is a sad fact that people can hear only 'Go and sin no more', without the other half, 'neither do I condemn you.' This needs to be acknowledged with sorrow by all within the Church. But one must remember that priests are imperfect because the whole Church is imperfect. The first people that should remember this are priests, but so should anyone inclined to cast a stone. Above all, do not give up on Jesus because of his ministers.

It seems fair to say, however, that much of the modern difficulty with confession is to do with the ministers. This is not a simple problem. The first manifestation is the priest who gets it all very wrong, who shouts and condemns. This is probably unforgivable for any who have been on the receiving end. I will admit to you candidly that a bad experience put me off the sacrament for some time. It is only recently, being privileged to hear confessions, that I have begun to recover a sense of grace at work in the sacrament. But it does not take a bad experience. Most of us are lucky enough to have friends to whom we can pour out our hearts and tell of our troubles. It is not clear that the rather 'clinical' rite of penance meets a need that is not fulfilled in other, more congenial ways. Friends, or counsellors, know me and we talk in a context that is sometimes lacking in a parish penance service.

A second-level problem is the priest who talks rhubarb. This can take a number of forms. Perhaps it is facile 'advice' from another, simpler world, the spiritual equivalent of expecting a drug addict to be free of his or her cravings by saying, 'Drugs are bad for you.' People often ask how a celibate man, protected from many of life's knocks, can expect to talk sense about the everyday problems of family life. Another, slightly less raw, form of rhubarb is what might be called 'ritual pronouncements'. You are given a little homily on preparing for Easter or whatever, and told to say one Our Father and two Hail Marys. The experience can be arid, a perfunctory anticlimax to all the careful preparation and steeling of nerves that can go into entering the confessional.

Both these sets of obstacles are minor, however, relative to the real issues. Let us note an important fact. Catholics, generally, do not go to confession. Those who do can often find it a difficult, stressful or unsatisfying ordeal. The best explanation is that the celebration of this sacrament does not satisfy a need. A harsh judgement would be that this is because we have lost our sense of need, our sense of sin, that we need to wake up to God and his commandments, realize by how much we fail, and return to the practice of penance in the hope of forgiveness. For some people, this is undoubtedly true, and there is a little of it in all of us. Few people actually want to admit what they have done wrong to themselves, still less to somebody else. The natural penitent is a rare beast, and not always a healthy one. Confession is difficult, because it means facing up to things we do not want to face.

A reason to try

Not facing them, however, leads to a constricted life. Suppose you live in a house with lots of rooms for every occasion. You have a bedroom, with ensuite shower and jacuzzi; you have several spare rooms for guests; there is a splendid garden, and a sitting room with French windows opening onto it for summer use; there is an oak-panelled dining room, and a more cheerful room for breakfast. The kitchen has all the latest devices and a well-stocked cellar. One day, you drop and break one of a pair of priceless Ming vases. After a while you get fed up staring at the one survivor; it is absurd on its own, and only reminds you of the stupid accident. So it gets banished to the basement. A few weeks later, you knock over the coffee table, breaking one of its legs. No glue is available, so you prop it up as best you can. But it is not really safe to take your splendid tea service, so you use the side table instead, and balance cups on the arms of people's chairs. Inevitably there are spillages and stains, and the room becomes rather tatty as time goes on. But there is no means of removing the blemishes, and you cannot afford another set of lovely antique furniture. You replace it with modern stuff, as good as you can get: metal tubes and leather. But it does not really fit the room, so you stop using it when you have guests.

An early Christian writer made the same point more succinctly:

> If we say we have no sin in us, we are deceiving ourselves and refusing to admit the truth; but if we acknowledge our sins, then God who is faithful and just will forgive our sins and purify us from everything that is wrong ... If anyone should sin, we have our advocate with the Father, Jesus Christ, who is just; he is the sacrifice that takes our sins away, and not only ours, but the whole world's.
>
> 1 John 1:8–9, 2:1–2

It is entirely possible to say that we have no sin. But is it true? Almost certainly not. If you say you have no sin, there is the question of how close you are to being the Pharisee; better to be a sinner than one of those. It is also entirely possible to know we have sin in us, but to brush it under some mental or spiritual carpet. This denial can happen in all kinds of ways: excuse-making, rewriting of history, blame of someone else, the didn't-mean-it-like-that defence, saying it was only a little thing, everyone does it from time to time, it doesn't hurt anyone else so why not, it was the most loving thing to do, there are limits, someone else should do it, why can't the government do its job and keep these people off the streets. But the most lethal ways of all are repentance and resolution. I do not mean real repentance and a genuine resolve to try to be better; these are holy, good, healing and often painfully cathartic. What I mean is an almost casual brushing away of things, saying you'll never do it again as a way of relieving entirely temporary feelings of guilt, gushing with sorrow as a way of avoiding retribution by others or by the angry god in your own head.

The trouble is that these lethal ways of living are very easy. They are easily disguised, and almost impossible to avoid. They are lethal because they dress up as the real thing and you have to get up very early indeed to catch them. But little by little, the small mound of unrepented sins gets bigger, sweep it under the carpet as you will. The carpet might easily be the sense that we have repented. After all, the Church teaches that sacramental confession is necessary only for mortal sins; with venial, everyday sins, we can be washed clean by simple contrition and prayer to God. That is true. But simple contrition is simply that – simple. How complex and self-interested, by comparison, is our desire to be free of guilt, to lose the fear of retribution, of bad luck, to feel that we are basically quite good people, after all. I can prove it; basically quite good people, who live without fear of retribution, who really believe that Jesus has taken away our sins, have no problem at all going to confession.

That will be explained in a moment. For now, back to the carpet. It is not easy to sweep an elephant under a carpet, and almost impossible to do so in such a way that nobody will notice the lump. It is, on the other hand, easy to sweep an ant under the carpet; or, indeed, a few hundred ants. But it only takes enough ants to make a pile the size of an elephant, and, of course, ants are easier to come by (and stamp on, so that they co-operate) than elephants. Half-repented little sins can wreck your life just as much as the one big mistake. It is easy to see how. Just as a series of small breakages, stains and bad memories can make a room uninhabitable, not to say a whole house, if nothing is done, so a series of small departures from the will of God can slowly put out all the lights in your heart.

We are working, if you remember, with a more grown-up idea of sin than as simply a transgression of a law code. Of course, as we have seen before, the law code is often a very good guide as to what might be sinful and what might not. But we have tried to understand the reality which the code roughly codifies. A life lived by the grace of God is something like a field of crops open to the sun and the rain, which are provided in just the right proportions and quantities. But, in practice, various things militate against the perfect harvest: poorly drained soil, insect or pigeon damage, invasions of hungry sheep. Anything you do which prevents the love of God coming to its fullest fruition in you can be called a sin. It can sometimes be as daft as holding up umbrellas to keep the rain off parched soil, but often it is more subtle and even misguided self-improvement.

The slope is slippery because sin deprives us of the life of God within us. That leaves a hole we are desperate to fill. And filled it gets, though not with the best things. Like the householder who cannot afford proper furniture, we fill our lives and souls up with junk, cadged from wherever we can get it, whatever we can afford. Of course, like much junk, it may be more comfortable. But does it last, is it better? More importantly, is it what you are really for? The furniture in the house is like all the bright gifts that God has put within each one of us. What do you do with yours? And what happens to them? Using the arm of a chair as a table for a hot drink is asking for trouble, as much as using food as a consolation to gorge yourself on, or drunken orgies as a substitute for love. Each step may seem sensible, a good temporary accommodation; after all, we are all human. But the whole place gets wrecked surprisingly easily. And God looks on, desperate to stop us being so stupid.

Finding a way

His hands are tied unless we let him in. This is the point of the sacrament of Reconciliation. It gives us a chance to admit to what is going on, to step back from it. In the words of St John, if we do admit that we have sin in us, then we find a God who is merciful and just, who has already forgiven us. All you have to do is accept his grace. Here is the reason for confession to a priest. It puts the sins 'outside' us, makes them objective, puts them openly on the table. Our own housekeeping is too superficial, too hurried and ultimately not up to the task. Left to ourselves we drift out of use as slowly and inexorably as a neglected sitting room.

And what a shame that is. The sacrament is not simply about wiping your slate. It is to do with how you relate, interconnect, with everyone else. If your bright gifts become tarnished, if the well-honed tools are used for things other than their purpose, you end up with botched jobs, damage, loss of facility. Just as you can no longer hold parties in the decayed room, you can no longer quite connect with people.

This is a sense that the Church is trying to recover in confession. Sin is not just a private affair between you and God, since it damages other people and the whole world. It does this not just by direct effect – like murdering someone – but also because as the flow of grace becomes restricted in you, God is less able to work through you to help and heal others. Hence, reconciliation is not just with God, but with other people, and we all need to be reconciled to each other more than we care to admit. The sacrament is a community event. Through it, we are healed, but so also is the Body of Christ that we have wounded. The New Rite of Penance, promulgated after Vatican II, tries to underline this with the possibility of communal celebrations, using readings, hymns and psalms, combined with individual confession.

It also contains a service called Rite III. This allows for full sacramental absolution to be given to a congregation *without* individual confession of sins to a priest. According to the book, this is only to be used in extreme circumstances such as danger of death (a plane crashing, troops going into combat) or in situations, for example in large mission territories, where there are not enough priests to hear the confessions of everyone in a reasonable time. For some, this seems to provide the way forward in other, 'normal' situations. Since people no longer relate to traditional confession for the reasons mentioned above, why not abandon it and extend the use of Rite III? That way, the faithful are not deprived of grace and forgiveness, but need not go through a fruitless, difficult and humiliating 'shopping list' of sins and peccadilloes in the presence of a priest who does not understand or worse. Yes, it is a retreat from the ideals of the confessional, but something is better than nothing. Some parishes now use Rite III as a matter of course.

Perhaps they are right, although the official Church does not agree. Something is indeed better than nothing. But individual aural confession holds out some possibilities that are not so easily fulfilled in a communal, easy, rite of penance. A moment ago I made a statement that may have enraged you. It was this: basically quite good people, who live without fear of retribution, who really believe that Jesus has taken away our sins, have no problem at all going to confession. You may have felt that as a judgement on you, a kind of innuendo implying that unless you go to confession, you must have something really, really wrong with you.

Well, you do. Everyone does. There have been very few human beings who find confession easy or even possible for the right reasons. Wrong reasons are plenty, including a kind of ritualist sense of being OK now, or a desire to feel holy, or a compulsion to think and say the worst about oneself. But none of us, deep down, really believes that God is pleased to see us. It is incredibly stupid. The man who repairs furniture would be delighted to see you with the damaged table; it is what he does for a living, and he wants to be helpful. God would be delighted if you turned up with your sins; forgiving is what he does for his living, and he wants to be helpful. Individual confession does just that, it puts our needs openly on the table, in the light, which means that God can actually do something about them.

But why a priest? Why do we have to do it? The priest, hard though it is to believe at times, is, for sacramental purposes, Christ himself. Every priest should weep daily at how far he falls short. Consider, though, the reasons we do not want to go. The priest won't understand; he will condemn; we feel small telling all our faults to someone else; our lives are too busy; our sins are only small, anyway; you just get a meaningless penance; it is unsatisfying, frightening. Compare that with how we tend to think of God: remote, wrathful, uninterested in us; we are just tiny cogs in a big universe; we can hide things from him by hiding them from ourselves; he is not part of the day-to-day grind, is interested only in holy things, good people. What rubbish – yet we all believe it! I think the point is clear. Every one of our actions matters to God as though it is the only thing done in the whole world, because each of us matters to God as though there were only us. At some level, our evasion of confession is an evasion of that fact. If you can, but only as you can, it is worth confronting that resistance. Here is the proof:

> During his life on earth, Jesus offered up prayer and entreaty, aloud and in silent tears, to the one who had the power to save him out of death, and he submitted so humbly that his prayer was heard. Although he was Son, he learned to obey through suffering, but having been made perfect, he became for all who obey him the source of eternal salvation.
>
> Hebrews 5:7–9

If he can do it, so can we. Because Christ shared our whole life, our whole life can be lived for and towards him. No sin is too small for him to desire with all his strength to bear it and to heal the consequences. Notice also the promise. Christ became for all who obey him a source of salvation. That is open to you too, to be a source of salvation to all you meet; simply because your every action, if offered to him, can become full of grace.

How to do it

A certain amount of discomfort, of bashfulness, is entirely natural to penance. It is appropriate, we are rightly ashamed. Many people get put off at this point, simply because they do not know what they are meant to do, like not going to a party in case you say the wrong thing. What a shame! At the same time, however, the decline in use of the sacrament of Reconciliation could actually be a source of encouragement. People flock to Rite III services, licit or not. That shows the depth of need for sacramental absolution. But they turn away from 'conventional' confession. This reflects a demand for something better than what we offer. The challenge is to find it, and to recover the sense that the Church really can meet the need. As hinted above, universal Rite III would be ducking this challenge. It is quite possible that we are returning to a more ancient pattern of infrequent but very careful and significant confessions at key moments of people's lives.

The renewed rites are not too far off what this implies, if they are done well and with courage. The context is scriptural and the structure otherwise close to the traditional rite. Many people are put off, feeling that they have nothing to say. That is something to say in itself. For in that case, you may not know yourself very well, and are maybe not in as close contact with the real world as you might be. If you have nothing to say, then presumably you do all you can already for those in need. You never walk past a homeless person without a smile and a prayer for them, you are constantly in intercession for an end to war across the globe, you love your neighbour as yourself and show that actively in more ways than can be counted ... Occasional use of the sacrament of Reconciliation can, slowly, open one's eyes to how one really is.

This is so on another front, just as important. The word 'confession' used to have two senses. It meant what it does now, admitting to the wrong one has done. But it also used to mean 'praise', praise of God for all he has done for you and does for you now. The sacrament is also a time to reflect on the good things we do with God's help, the ways we truly reflect the image of Christ in the world. If you cannot see any of those as you read this, then you really do need to do an examination of conscience.

This horrible phrase, 'examination of conscience', does not do justice to what is an opportunity to take stock of one's life, and see where it is leading and why. It does not do justice to the opportunity to face long-buried hurts and resentments, to face up to demons within. It need not be anything dramatic. If you feel that your sins are too boring and humdrum to bother God with, then this betrays an inner reluctance to let him close to you on the level of detail. You are happy to have Jesus in church, but not at the breakfast table. But that is exactly where he wants to be. Let him in, don't be afraid.

Young couples, or very close friends, find that the only way they can bear being apart is to know what the other is doing at that moment (mobile phones are so useful here!) or, when they meet, to extract from each other a precise account of the day. The tragedy is when people do not have time to do this, or feel resentful of the demands made by another person being that interested in them. But hold on a minute! Is that not what we most want, someone who cares that much? Christ is there, and desperately interested in your day because of his unfathomable interest in you. Share it, and see it taken up into the conversation of the Trinity itself.

In the renewed rite, confession begins with a greeting in which the priest makes you welcome and tries to help you relax. You then share a passage of scripture, which you or he can choose, or take a set one. You pray together for the grace of God to help you free yourself of your burden, then discuss together what is on your mind. The priest may have some advice which is helpful, or just some encouragement not to give up. He gives you a penance which should be some kind of help, rather than just a token punishment. For example, if you are troubled by a tendency to think nasty thoughts about other people, he may suggest you spend a few minutes praying for someone you don't like. Then you express your sorrow for sin, and your hope one day to be free of it, and he says those beautiful words of absolution with which we began. Why not give it a try?

Chapter 10

EYE OF THE NEEDLE

See I set before you today a blessing and a curse.

Deuteronomy 11:26

Most people are aware of the statement of Jesus that it is easier for a camel to pass through the eye of a needle than for a rich person to enter the kingdom of God. His disciples' reaction to this might mirror our own: what about us? On this line, how can anyone be saved? Jesus answers that, for God, everything is possible; perhaps the most unsatisfactory reply in all four Gospels.

But let's be realistic – at least for a moment. We live as part of a complex global economy; our societies are deeply interdependent for raw materials and finished products. Without American grain and Polish coal the system would collapse, and we would have little to eat and nothing to eat it with. Such things have to be exchanged, which means money and tokens of value. You buy somebody some flowers as you go to visit them in hospital. Is such an action doomed because it involves money? Human life, as we know it, cannot proceed without possessions and ways of exchanging them. Jesus is not on the same planet.

It is always possible with Jesus' more difficult sayings that they are meant to be difficult. Suppose he said something like, 'If you have a lot of money, then you should remember to help the poor; after all, you can't take it with you ...' Well, we know that already, and it passes us by, or not. It has little impact, does not grab one's attention. But to say that a camel has more chance of squeezing through the eye of a needle than a rich man of being saved is to invite shocked incredulity. Where does one draw the line?

Obviously, billionaires are out, but what about people with just a house and a car? Maybe he means we should just have what we need. But what one person needs to survive in the Western world is enough for many to live on in other parts of the world. Even if we are sure of ourselves in this matter, we are still part of an economic structure that seems inherently disordered.

This raises the question as to why it is disordered, what might have gone wrong. It is not hard for us to imagine a society in which all have what they need and no more, in which surpluses are shared equally for the common good. Essential services are provided communally and fairly. Nobody is in want, and there is a little extra for those who have earned it to enjoy. Nor is it hard for us to imagine how long that would actually last. The reason any attempt at creating ideal states or economic conditions has always ended up as a dictatorship is that human beings do not naturally share. Inevitably somebody will want something they have not got, and will be prepared to take steps to get it. In the best case, this turns into a market economy in which people barter what they need for what other people want. But history is strewn with worse cases.

We have looked at some of the questions that this raises in chapter 6. It is very hard for a Christian to say, as many do, that religion and politics are different things. This denial is very old, and the New Testament authors found reason to quarrel with it:

> If one of the brothers or one of the sisters is in need of clothes and has not enough food to live on, and one of you says to them, 'I wish you well; keep yourself warm and eat plenty', without giving them these bare necessities of life, then what good is that? Faith is like this; if good works do not go with it, it is quite dead.
>
> James 2:15–16

It is very easy to say that the Church should keep out of politics, that social teaching is just lefty rubbish propounded by soft liberals – if you have somewhere to live, and enough to eat.

Take a closer look

But it is a foolish thing to say, because the disorder of the world outside you is the reflection of the disorder within you. People starve because other people are greedy; thousands of refugees flee conflicts created by restless human antagonism which refuses to forgive. If you do not play your part in healing what is outside, then what is within you is put beyond God's grace. But if you are torn within by the suffering that you see, then know that your own salvation is at hand:

> Just as the person fully realizes himself in the free gift of self, so too ownership morally justifies itself in the creation, at the proper time and in the proper way, of opportunities for work and human growth for all.
>
> John Paul II, *Centesimus Annus*, 43

The proof of that is in the life of Jesus, someone far richer than any of us will ever be, who became poor even to death, and rose again. By his self-emptying he won for us the chance to give of ourselves and so become ourselves, truly, in God's likeness. Few of us come close to a complete gift of self. But we try, and for God that is more than a start. He will complete it. As Mother Teresa famously commented, 'the ocean is made up of drops'. Stand back, if you wish, and maybe hide your reluctance to reach out under some convenient ideological banner. You will be the loser, because you will miss the chance to grow in faith and hope and love by sharing with Christ the burden of our sin.

Catholic morality is optimistic about humanity. It is never, ever condemnatory. The commandments, after all, are part of God's plan of redemption. They are ways back to him, not ways of making mistakes. A good example of how it works is in the shortest of St Paul's letters, to Philemon, one of his converts who lived near Ephesus. The letter is a worked example of the disorientation into which the Gospel casts what we thought were straightforward relationships, how it challenges what our culture and human nature tells us are our obvious and manifest rights, what is politically sensible and economically feasible, and all the other nonsense we hide behind when we want to deny the truth about other people. Paul is writing because one of Philemon's slaves, called Onesimus, has run away from his master and sought refuge at the other end of the Mediterranean with Paul in Rome. He wants Philemon to grant Onesimus his freedom.

This is nuts. Under Roman law, you were entitled to punish a runaway slave by branding. In practice, the master could do almost anything he felt appropriate, and with harsh masters that would mean hard labour intended to kill. On the other hand, a good slave who had served well for some time might receive his 'freedom'; it would then take a couple of generations before his offspring would be free of the stigma of slavery and able to relate as something like equals to their former masters. Paul's request, in that world, is outrageous: 'I know you have been deprived of Onesimus for a time, but it was only so that you could have him back for ever, not as a slave any more but as a dear brother in the Lord' (Philemon 15). Not only must Philemon set Onesimus free as his punishment for running away, but he must treat him as a blood-brother. To accept Onesimus as a fellow Christian, as someone equally a human being, would have strained Philemon's faith to its limits. Unfortunately, we don't have his answer to Paul (perhaps it was not printable), so we do not know what happened. What we do know is that it took over eighteen hundred Christian years before a Christian country abolished slavery.

It was Philemon who needed to be set free, not Onesimus. It is not the starving who need food, but we who need hunger. It is we who need to be set free from the sin that clings to us and blinds us from knowing and choosing what is good. How does it happen? Jesus says, 'Love your enemies, do good to those who persecute you.' If that is our way out of the mire then we are lost; well, I'm lost, anyway, you may be fine. God does not command in order to torment us, but in order to save. The teachings of Christ as to how we should live are invitation, not demand. They are a description of what God will give us and do in us, if we let him.

And the way we let him is to open ourselves to thinking that when God forbids or commands something, he may have a point. It is to believe that God desires not our failure, but our good. It is to believe that in giving we receive. We know this is true, despite our best instincts, because of what God has done already. Across the vast distance we put between ourselves and him, he has sent his own message, in the life and death of his Son. But Jesus does better than Philemon. He does not just accept us as penitent runaways, give us our freedom and treat us as friends. He comes to find us in our thicket of fallen loves, and home, rejoicing, will bear us.

Over to you

That is the ideal, and it sounds pretty good. But what about the practice? God has entrusted this process to the human Church, which means you, and me too, I suppose. Much of the finding and carrying, on the practical level, is given to us to do. Here is where we cannot refuse social responsibility, no matter how much we would like to. The devil, and Western culture, do their best to persuade us that if we give, we will be the losers. But either this is not true, or the Gospel is not true:

> Give, and there will be gifts for you, a full measure, pressed down, shaken together, and running over, will be poured into your lap; because the amount you measure out is the amount you will be given back.
>
> Luke 6:38

Pope Leo XIII in his 1891 encyclical, *Rerum Novarum* ('New Things'), attacked the distinction between this-world and other-world, between faith and politics, the idea that religion is solely a 'spiritual' thing to do with experience of personal piety. What has been said above is intended to give an incentive for overcoming such a distinction in one's own life. The same encyclical set out for the first time some of the implications of Christianity for economic and social life. It was immensely influential, and you can find in Leo's thought grounding for much modern talk of human rights and international law, not to mention the UN Declaration on Human Rights. He was addressing a bitterly divided society – divided between rich and poor, between capitalist and worker, between revolutionists and reactionaries. He warned of what would follow if such divisions were not healed by a new vision of human dignity. Nobody listened, of course, and much of the sad story of the twentieth century has been as Leo predicted.

The Gospel has real consequences; the Church has a real contribution to make to discussions of economic and social policy, as well as in guiding us on how to live our lives in the sight of God. However, this cannot and should not be identified with any one political party or dogma. The papal campaign against communism in the 1980s was not a vindication of the Reagan and Bush programmes. Since the Church bears the Word of God to the world, it cannot be limited within any political system. The basic principle that the Church seeks to communicate is that amidst all the calls of wealth, convenience and supply, human beings have a capacity for transcendence, that within and without the material world is a meaning and a blessing of God who made it, that each human being is a person loved by God with unique dignity.

If that sounds abstract, it grounds all kinds of human rights from the right to work to the right to form trade unions and have reasonable leisure. It is put concretely in the following three brief extracts from Leo's *Rerum Novarum*, extracts which show how far ahead of its time it was:

> No man may with impunity violate that human dignity which God himself treats with great reverence.
>
> 126

> It is neither just nor human so to grind men down with excessive labour as to stupefy their minds and wear out their bodies.
>
> 128

> The State is bound to protect natural rights, not to destroy them; and if it forbids its citizens to form associations, it contradicts the very principle of its own existence.
>
> 135

Thinking like this allows one to tell the wood from the trees, and what is an absolute right from what is only relative to the needs of others. If your teenager demands an absolute right to use the telephone, you would counter with the suggestion that family finances and patience have to be taken into account. For example, private property is a right. But not of itself. We have a right to possess things for the sake of our welfare and that of our family, in so far as that does not deprive another person and their family unjustly.

Similarly, every economic or social decision, whether it is on the level of great nations or of you deciding which brand of ice cream to buy, has to take into account the way it affects the human race as a whole. If it sounds absurd to say that, rather than thinking about the colour of a shirt, one should worry about the conditions in which workers produced it, then it is also absurd to say that the *people* who work in the sweatshops matter more than the impression you make at the party. Consumers have vast choice, enormous power. Even huge multinationals can be brought to their knees by ordinary people like you and me refusing to be implicated in what they do.

This should not be confused with a world-denying glorification of primitive poverty or backwardness. The Church does not idealize any past time as did, for example, the movement centred around Eric Gill in England early in the last century which tried to live without machines as a way of resisting the inevitable advance of industrial society. That is not right, simply because it is so pessimistic about humanity. Catholics are optimistic about people because we know what they could be if only they knew who they really are. This right to development and progress is itself a fundamental moral good. John Paul II notes, commenting on Leo's encyclical:

> The fact is that many people, perhaps the majority today, do not have the means which would enable them to take their place in an effective and humanly dignified way within a productive system in which work is truly central. They have no possibility of acquiring the basic knowledge which would enable them to express their creativity and develop their potential. They have no way of entering the network of knowledge and intercommunication which would enable them to see their qualities appreciated and utilised. Thus, if not actually exploited, they are to a great extent marginalized.
>
> *Centesimus Annus*, 33

This is not a call for the kind of hamburger imperialism that has characterized Western attempts to spread prosperity around the globe, but for a simple respect of other people and what their culture has to offer.

It is not wrong to want to live better, or in comfort. It is wrong to lose sight of the reasons for living in the first place. There is much we cannot do, and much that we have not the courage to try. But if we hoard what we have, for the sake of enjoying it, refuse to share even a little, then it is we who become poor. The final tragedy is when we do not even know it. The eye of the needle is only as small as is your vision of the worth of your fellow humans. For God, and for those who try to live by his truth, everything is possible. Much has already been done, even in two millennia. Philemon is not yet free, but he has begun to unclench his fist.

Of course, he is not expected to do it all on his own. Jesus did not simply give us a set of objectives with no place to work them out. He also founded a Church, which he meant to be a community in which all could find their salvation by helping each other and serving all people. Has it worked out? Is the Church more of a hindrance than a help? Should we look for other ways, or should we try and reform the Church? If so, how? The background to answering some of these questions is the subject of the next section. First we look at what the Church is meant to be, and then at some of the problems Catholics encounter in being that kind of Church.

PART 3

THE CHURCH AND US

Chapter 11

MEETING CHRIST

Wherever you go, I will go.

Ruth 1:16

Meeting Christ is the point of it all, the reason for the existence of the Church: that Christ may walk the path of life with each person. Even so, one might complain that God has not chosen the best way to go about revealing himself. The Church is more often today a source of scandal and something to excuse and apologize for than something to admire and venerate. Or is that fair? In fact, it is not fair, nor accurate, and is based on a misconception, not surprisingly the same misconception we are meeting all along. To make things clearer, let us look right back to the foundation of the Church.

> Peter spoke up, 'You are the Christ,' he said, 'the Son of the living God.' Jesus replied, 'Simon, son of Jonah, you are a happy man! Because it was not flesh and blood that revealed this to you but my Father in heaven. So I now say to you: You are Peter and on this rock I will build my Church. And the gates of the underworld can never hold out against it. I will give you the keys of the kingdom of heaven: whatever you bind on earth shall be considered bound in heaven; whatever you loose on earth shall be considered loosed in heaven.'
>
> (Matthew 16:16–20)

Scholars like to haggle over exactly what Jesus meant by this, especially the word 'Church'. It is unlikely that he was understood to mean the Church as we have it now, a vast and complex enterprise. But on the other hand we cannot show what he did or didn't mean or that he did or did not actually say any or all of it. For better or worse, this text has become the foundation charter for the long Roman adventure with all its many bursts of light and moments of darkness. Let us ponder for a while what it means to us who live in the current episode.

In particular, the choice of Simon Peter is not accidental. What qualifies him to be singled out as the rock on which it will come to be built? In the story, he has just had a revelation, a vision of who Jesus really is. He is often singled out for such experiences. With James and John, he witnesses the Transfiguration and the agony of Gethsemane; he has his own special meeting with the risen Christ. But these are peaks in a land of valleys. Most often, he is with the other disciples, full of misunderstanding, arrogance or hardness of heart. Sometimes he is in a league of his own, as when he denies Jesus in his hour of need, or when he sinks into the Sea of Galilee, having discovered that his faith is not so strong as he thought. The most sensible thing he says in all four Gospels is perhaps, 'Leave me, Lord, for I am a sinful man' (Luke 5:9). But even that was beside the point.

Start as you mean to continue

Was it an error of judgement, a moment of wild optimism, a poor joke for Jesus to call such a man a 'rock' and to found his Church on him? Let us consider, very briefly, the story of that Church. It began, as we know, badly. The disciples were a long way off understanding what Jesus was up to, and equally far off when it came to crucifixion. They responded with, at best, fearful joy to the news of resurrection. Time in Jerusalem was spent locked in a secret room for fear of persecution. Then Jesus gave them something to be really frightened of:

> As the Father sent me, so am I sending you. Receive the Holy Spirit. For those whose sins you forgive, they are forgiven; for those whose sins you retain, they are retained.
>
> John 20:21–2

In John's Gospel, the response of the disciples is to return to fishing in Galilee, and who could blame them? The vocation Jesus offered them is a daunting one. It is to be his presence in the world, the sign and reality of God's saving love, forgiving and retaining sins. Not until they were dynamited out of the Upper Room by the coming of the Holy Spirit at Pentecost did the disciples truly become apostles, preaching the good news to all nations and people.

Disputes arose immediately, however, over the problem of non-Jewish converts. You can see the controversy which split and splintered the newborn Church reflected vividly in the letters of the upstart Paul. This man, a persecutor turned convert, displayed all the usual disturbing, and sometimes unconstructive, characteristics of converts: enthusiasm, a conviction of being right, intolerance of other views, whether more cautious or daring than his. Several of the founding apostles apparently held that non-Jews must become Jews before they could be Christians. Paul, in his Spirit-driven mission across the whole Roman Empire, found that the situation on the ground did not square with this; his gentile converts received the Holy Spirit without circumcision or abstaining from pork. Sheer weight of numbers eventually settled the issue on Paul's side.

Once it was large enough to be noticed, the Church became persecuted. This had a number of causes. Either Christians were associated with the perennially unpopular Jews in pagan eyes, or else the Christian refusal to take part in state sacrifices, especially the emperor cult, was seen as undermining imperial rule, as rebellious and inviting the wrath of the gods on the Romans. Persecution was sporadic and locally organized, although there were several waves of official suppression ordered by the emperors. Christians could be killed, sometimes very savagely, property confiscated, and the houses in which they met, furtively and fearfully, burned down. And the Church flourished. As the second-century writer Tertullian put it, addressing the imperial authorities:

> Go on, then! The people will think you excellent magistrates if you sacrifice Christians to them. Torture us, rack us, condemn us, crush us – your cruelty proves our innocence. But you accomplish nothing else. The more you mow us down, the more of us there are; the blood of the martyrs is the seed of the Church.
>
> *Apology*, 50, slightly paraphrased

But persecution also created problems for the Christians. Chief among these were those who lapsed under the pressure. If you were given the choice between renouncing Christ and being fed to a lion for the entertainment of the people next door, which would you

choose? Many could not but accept martyrdom, and we still venerate their memory: Cecilia, Lucy, Laurence, Ignatius, Justin, and
most of the apostles are just a few among thousands. But others,
understandably, failed the test and gave in. They were sometimes
persuaded to denounce other Christians or to betray hiding places.
The problem was how the Church should regard such people.
Some said that if you had publicly lapsed and renounced Christ,
that was it, you were out. Others were for taking them back with full
forgiveness and an attempt to rebuild trust. This heroic attitude
eventually resulted in a compromise: people could return to the
Church community by following a ritual of public penance, leading up to reconciliation, usually at Easter. But the compromise did
not hold everywhere. The fifth-century North African bishop, St
Augustine, engaged literally in guerilla warfare with a separated
group called the Donatists who held to a hard line, and tried to
enforce it by a mix of intimidation and preaching.

By Augustine's time, Christianity was established and
respectable. It had become the official religion of the Roman
Empire with the conversion of the emperor Constantine in about
315, and quickly began to build churches and acquire all the other
marks of settling down, including using the imperial resources to
stamp out paganism. Such a position of security was a mixed blessing. Along with the obvious advantages there was a gradual lessen-
ing of fervour. Many converts became Christian for purposes of
career advancement or simply because that was how the world was.
It is not far from the situation in England since the sixteenth century, in which everyone is a nominal Anglican unless there is strong
evidence to the contrary. And just as the active section of the
Church of England is alive and healthy today, so the newly tolerated Church had a large core of genuine Christians of conviction and
courage. Out of these grew the monastic movement and, eventually, the explosion of missionary activity through the Dark Ages.

But the inevitable dumbing-down process did lower the stan-
dards of Christian life. Once again the Church became split over
the question of sins committed after baptism. Some, among them
a British monk called Pelagius, held that Jesus' commandments
were all possible if only we took them seriously and tried hard
enough; since perfection was possible, we are all obliged to it.
History decided against Pelagianism. Thinkers like Augustine drew
attention to our apparently inevitable bias to sin and compromise.

The Church was seen as a way of dealing with this, in the sacraments, leading people gradually back into being the image of God. St Benedict, writing for his sixth-century monks, summed up this model of Christian community, its aims and effects, thus:

> The monk will quickly arrive at that perfect love of God which casts out fear. Through this love, all that he once performed with dread, he will now begin to observe without effort, as though naturally, from habit, no longer out of fear of hell, but out of love for Christ, good habit and delight in virtue.
>
> *Rule*, Prologue

This is a very particular way of looking at life, and hence at the Church. In the face of Christians who, though themselves sincere and authentic in their faith, put the standard of life as high as perfection, a different vision of Christianity gradually emerged. A good Christian is a bad person who is not afraid to admit it, who knows that God never takes back his gifts or revokes his choice. Similarly, for Benedict, a good monk is a bad person who longs to hear Christ say, 'my friend, come up higher' (Luke 14:10). From this comes Christian community, a group of people who can be open about their own needs and forgiving of those of others. There is no smugness, no sense of being the right kind, the right place. Jesus is in the midst of them, for he is welcome, desperately wanted.

In this context, the choice of that crumbly, unstable and dubious rock, St Peter, to be our foundation, begins to make some sense. Jesus chose Simon to be the rock, because he had a very clear idea of what the Church was going to be like; what, in fact, it is like now. I have described just one fault line in the Christian community, and traced it only for the first few centuries. There are many others, and they extend even into our time. Why? Because they are in us. They are in you and me. The tensions of the Church arise because of the tensions in each Christian. The Church is intolerant because you and I are intolerant. The Church is worldly because I am worldly; it is political and divided because I am ambitious and divisive. The Church is judgemental because I condemn people in my heart. The Church is human, because it is made up of people like me.

But that is not all. Jesus looked at Simon, knew him through and through. He knows you and me just as well. He has given each of us a name in our baptism, and has said, in different ways to each, 'on you will I build my Church'. The terrible mandate given to the disciples is ours too; it has application to sacramental authority, but also a more general meaning. If you forgive sin, it is forgiven; if you retain sin, you bind Christ's hands. He cannot dispel our hate because he has given that power to us. He has given to us the message and task of reconciliation.

It is up to you and me to lead the world back to its Creator, to live in such a way that within our small spheres of influence Christ may walk with each person the path of life. This imposes a certain way of living which tells us much about the nature of the Church, and how to cope with it.

> The Church, if she is to be *reconciling*, must begin by being a reconciled Church ... In order ever more effectively to proclaim and propose reconciliation to the world, the Church must become ever more genuinely a community of disciples of Christ (even though it were only 'the little flock' of the first days), united in the commitment to be continually converted to the Lord and to live as new people in the spirit and practice of reconciliation ...
>
> And for this purpose we must all work to bring peace to people's minds, to reduce tensions, to overcome divisions and to heal wounds ... in accordance with the ancient maxim: In what is doubtful, freedom; in what is necessary, unity; in all things, charity.
>
> John Paul II, *Reconciliatio et Paenitentia*, 9

The first witness of the Church is to human sin, to our need of Christ and his love. Such a witness can normally be taken for granted. But its interpretation to the world requires constant effort and a return to essentials. The Church is a place, if any such place exists anywhere, where sins can be forgiven. We have all received the fullness of Christ, grace in return for shame. We receive it from each other, give it to each other. It is not surprising that the Church is a mess, has always been a mess. The surprise is that God works in it, in us. The community of sinners which is the Church is a sign of hope as well as of contradiction.

> I give you a new commandment: love one another; just as I have loved you, you also must love one another. By this love you have for one another, everyone will know that you are my disciples.
>
> John 13:35

Love contains tolerance, not tidiness. It involves forgiveness, not being right. It dictates respect, not judgement. And it tells me that the task of giving way, of going an extra mile, is not just 'theirs' but mine also. As the Father sent Christ to bear our faults without complaint, so he sends you.

We are not alone

The Church is bigger than it looks. One of the tasks of the novices in my monastery is to tend the cemetery: cut the grass, sweep leaves, prune bushes and so on. It is not always a gloomy or miserable task, even in North Yorkshire weather. There is a sense of knowing where I will end up one day. Less morbid is the thought of the many monks who have lived before me, who are part of my monastic family, whose influence lives on.

We all know, and most of us mourn, people who have died 'in the peace of Christ', even if not necessarily as Christians. It is hard to know what we are meant to think about death. To lose a husband, a wife, a brother, a sister, child or friend is the most shattering experience anyone can ever face. There is shock, there is often guilt, and an appalling depth of sadness. Either that, or we are numb, without feeling; more or less denying what has happened.

And then you have to learn to live with the memories. When my mother died a couple of years ago, my father was offered lots of well-meant advice about the so-called 'grief process', how he would feel this and feel that, and then gradually come to terms with the loss. He said, 'I don't want to get over this. I don't want it to be as though she never was.' Anniversaries, birthdays, places, even types of food and weather bring back memories of when one's loved one was alive. It is like a big hole; someone not sitting there. The fact that life goes on, and the pain fades to the extent that you cannot remember what people looked like, just adds another level of loss and confusion.

When my mother died I read a lot of self-help books, trying to find out how I should be feeling, and got plenty of advice from friends. Some of them talked about a grief process with stages; some encouraged one to 'talk about it'. Some were concerned that I should grieve healthily, but were not sure what that meant. Most of what I heard did not touch me at all. This is perhaps the important point; grief is private and unique. Nobody else had exactly the relation to your loved one that you did; even sisters or brothers have different life stories with respect to a mother or father. There is no period after which you should be 'through it', because there is no 'it' to go through or be 'over'. A death leaves a hole, a wound, a lost limb. Virtually anything goes as a reaction to this, except pretending that nothing has happened. And it is never over. Grief returns unexpected, though it can become welcome if you think of it as love. In particular, do not think you have lost your faith; it is simply buried or in ashes with your lost one.

Christian faith can be a help, and it can be a hindrance. I am sure I am not the only one who has wondered, in the face of bereavement, what to make of the consolation of religion. How does the feeling of despair, or sadness, relate to the gospel of the Resurrection? Should I not be overcome with joy that my dead relatives and friends have gone to live again with God? Is grief not a selfish indulgence, because all I can think of is what they meant to me? There seems a dishonesty somewhere; our hearts are black, when we should be wearing white.

When we remember our deceased relatives and friends, something extraordinary is going on. Look at all the things they gave us. Parents give us life; children give us hope; friends give us love; big sisters or little brothers give us all sorts of things we are not necessarily grateful for at the time. But in our remembrance of them, in our prayer for them, they give us something much greater. They are with Christ, and when we look towards them in gratitude or in sorrow, we look towards him as well.

The death of a loved one brings that choice home to us. The remembrance of them keeps alive in us the hope of something that cannot be clearly expressed. There is a Christian grief that is full of sorrow and full of hope. It becomes sadness not that the dead are no longer here with us, but that we are not yet there with them, where God wipes away every tear. When we pray for our family and friends who have died, it is in fact they who give to us. They give the remembrance that Christ is all in all, and that he is drawing us to himself, from whom all good things come.

It is such thinking that leads us to talk of the communion of saints. The only difference between any of the holy souls and a canonized saint is of degree of witness. The saints in the calendar are chosen by the Church because they illustrated in their lives a particular aspect of God's love and forgiveness. This, as we know, also means that they witnessed to a particular aspect of human weakness and sin. A saint is a sinner who lives before God with confidence in him. For this reason we pray to them for help and inspiration. The eucharistic preface in the liturgy for a saint's day sums it up well:

> You are glorified in your saints, for their glory is the crowning of your gifts. In their lives on earth, you give us an example. In our communion with them, you give us their friendship. In their prayer for the Church you give us strength and protection. This great company of witnesses spurs us on to victory, to share their prize of everlasting glory, through Jesus Christ our Lord.

Our Lady

Foremost among the saints is the Virgin Mary. Catholic thinking about her has often been misunderstood, especially by Catholics, and can sometimes be confused or confusing. It has to be admitted that some of the things which Catholics say about Our Lady sound very strange indeed to modern ears: conceived immaculate, free from original sin; assumed, body and soul, into heaven at her death; mother, yet ever-virgin; appearing all over the world with bizarre and sometimes very political messages. In an area like this the traditional tag is very helpful – in what is doubtful, freedom; in what is necessary, unity; in all things, charity. None of us has a right to dismiss another's piety, even when it seems far-fetched or even childish. Nor should anyone criticize another for 'insufficient devotion'. Particular care needs to be taken by crusaders in this or any other area of faith not to raise a personal or national devotion to the level of an infallible doctrine. The Christian Gospel does not stand or fall on whether the Medjugorje apparitions are genuine, though the faith of individuals can be rightly and healthily tied up with such belief. Marian piety need not be morbid, but nor need it be aggressive. On the other hand, there are doctrines the Catholic faith does stand or fall by and these, where they refer to the Virgin Mary, are fairly clearly identified. They include immaculate conception, virgin birth, assumption.

Why insist on these, when there is so much to be said, theologically and historically, against them, when they can be a source of so much misunderstanding and, indeed, obstacles to unity with other, more squeamish, Christians? The reason lies in the nature of the Church which Christ founded. This point was well made by the Fathers of the Second Vatican Council in 1964 when they spoke about Mary at the conclusion of their statement about the Church, *Lumen Gentium*. They saw Our Lady as part of the Church, not above it; as one of us, not some kind of semi-goddess. But she has become, by the grace of God, a sign of where we are all heading if we listen to God's call of love.

> While in the most Blessed Virgin the Church has already reached ... perfection ... the faithful still strive to conquer sin and increase in holiness. And so they turn their eyes to Mary who stands forth to the whole community of the elect as the model of virtues.
>
> *Lumen Gentium*, 65

How is she the model of virtues? Because she said 'yes' to God, willingly bore his Son, stayed close to him even when she did not understand, or when his life – and hers – had come to despair. As a result, she can still show us to him, just as any saint, or any of your own dead loved ones, but in the highest degree possible to humanity. The Council document continues:

> Having entered deeply into the history of salvation, Mary, in a way, unites in her person and re-echoes the most important doctrines of the faith: and when she is the subject of preaching and worship she prompts the faithful to come to her Son, to his sacrifice and to the love of the Father.
>
> *Lumen Gentium*, 65

She shows us, in fact, what you and I will be one day if we follow her example of openness to God in each other. That is to be truly a disciple of Christ, a member of his Church, a Catholic worthy of the name.

The Catholic Church is therefore much less than it looks, but also much more than it looks. It is this, often fractious, community of sinners which is slowly evolving into the communion of saints.

'Evolving slowly' because human beings change only slowly. The Holy Spirit knows, as we do too sometimes, that it is easy to break the pot in our eagerness to clean it. The vision of the Church expounded in this chapter, as it is expounded in the Church's own teaching, may perhaps seem to you a different Church entirely to the one we have, whose rough and craggy authority can seem harsh and indifferent to our real lives and real problems. But the vision is how the Church could be. To get there, we simply have to start to live the gospel vision, to be the first to forgive, the last to condemn, to live, in fact, in the hope that God's kingdom will come, and come even in our lifetime.

Chapter 12

HOW TO DISAGREE WITH THE POPE

I shall let my embittered soul speak out.

Job 10:2

The Pope is the most prominent feature of the Catholic Church. Rome and the papacy have dominated European and world history since the conversion of the Roman Empire in the fourth century. More recently, John Paul II is credited with a key part in the collapse of communism in Eastern Europe. The Pope speaks and is heard, if not listened to, on every contemporary issue of importance, from architecture to third world debt. In structural terms, he is the focus and source of unity of a huge organization across the world. But, more importantly, he is for Catholics the bishop of Rome, successor to St Peter, Vicar or representative of Christ on earth.

Apostolic succession is essential to Catholicism. It is impossible to show historically that there has been an unbroken line of popes going back to St Peter, because the evidence simply does not survive; there is very little evidence surviving from antiquity generally. Nor can one be completely sure about what Jesus meant when he gave primacy to Peter among the apostles. But, even if the early papal lists are wrong as to names and dates, we can be sure that there was *someone* functioning as Rome's bishop, and that Rome, from very early on, had a first place of honour in the growing Church because of its association with St Peter and St Paul.

The structure of the early Church was rather looser than it is now, however, and it is this fact which has fed one of the reforms (or renewals or rediscoveries, according to taste) of the Second

Vatican Council. The Church grew up roughly like this. Wandering preachers, of whom St Paul is the most famous and successful example, would visit towns and cities telling people about Jesus and his Gospel. After some time, he would move on, leaving behind one of his team, or one of his new converts, to look after the young community. Inevitably, problems arose that needed settling, and either the original apostle or the deputy on the ground would have to try and decide what the Gospel response should be. The point of the decision was that it was apostolic. It was not that whoever happened to be in charge made the decisions but that in resolving conflicts or dealing with new or unforeseen challenges the Christian community naturally turned to Christ, in prayer and communal discernment, but also in the person of the one who had first represented him to them.

Over time, two things happened. First, the consciousness that all the churches were joined together grew and deepened, and the idea of being in communion was developed. For an early snapshot of this in action, see the third letter of St John. Next, into the second and third generation men were chosen to succeed the original leaders; they acquired the title of *episkopos*, or overseer, which is translated into English as 'bishop'. You knew you were part of Christ's Body if you were in communion with your bishop who was in communion with all the other bishops, because your bishop could trace back an unbroken line of witness to the original apostles. After quite a short time, the focus of the communion of bishops became the bishop of Rome.

That is, of course, some way from papal infallibility or papal monarchy, the idea that the Pope alone supremely rules the Church, although these ideas were also present in embryonic form quite early. As soon as the Gospel became applied to life and Christians started bringing to the apostolic faith everyday questions of concern or interest, it became richer and more complicated in its expression. This meant, of course, that you could go very wrong indeed. We saw one particularly lethal example back in chapter 2.

If you *can* go wrong, you want to know what is right, and so the Church developed means to ensure that the truth, and not a convenient or clever substitute, was being taught. The principal means were councils and synods. The idea arose that all the bishops, meeting solemnly in a council, could by listening to each other and debating openly and honestly, reach the truth in question. More local questions could be decided by smaller, less grand, synods. A voice which was heard very seriously was that of the bishop of Rome, who always sent two representatives to a council.

Such collective decision making became rather obscured in later centuries. This was not through any particular fault, but just the way history went, and the Church responded to the changing times. In a world such as medieval Europe, for example, which was ruled by kings absolutely, it was natural for Church government to come to reflect this pattern. As always, the crooked lines of the Church tended to be the crooked lines of humanity in general and only long hindsight can tell which lines are indeed crooked and which straight. The elevation of the Pope into an independent decision maker has continued into our time. But one must not simply be scandalized by this. The papal office is a Church office, a ministry within the Church. It exists only because we look to it in order to find Christ; or, rather, it is a way Christ has given us to find him in time of doubt. There are other ways, but this way is sure and given by him. The Pope exists as pope as a focus of the whole Church; we produce him, make him. He is the expression, as well as the cause, of our unity in Christ. John Paul II put it like this:

> If one wants to refer to the dignity of the Bishop of Rome, one cannot consider it apart from the dignity of the entire college of bishops, with which it is tightly bound, as it is to the dignity of each bishop, each priest, and each of the baptized ... I would suggest a reading of Saint Augustine, who often repeated 'I am a bishop for you, I am a Christian with you'. On reflection, 'Christian' has far greater significance than 'bishop', even if the subject is the Bishop of Rome.
>
> *Crossing the Threshold of Hope*, 14

The ministry of the Pope is a collegial ministry; it is exercised with and for all the other bishops, and with and for each and every Catholic. So many people, praying earnestly and without self-interest to find the will of God and his truth, cannot go wrong if there really is a Holy Spirit. Remember it is not just the visible Church that is involved, but all those who have gone before, right back to the apostles themselves. This is what we mean by infallibility. It is not that if we must sink, let us sink together; it is that if we hold together we will not sink. Such a conception has become reinforced by the regular holding of synods of bishops in Rome to look at particular questions, after which the Pope writes an Apostolic Exhortation. It works along the lines envisaged by the Second Vatican Council:

> Although the individual bishops do not enjoy the prerogative of infallibility, they do nevertheless proclaim Christ's doctrine infallibly even when dispersed around the world, provided that, while maintaining the bond of communion among themselves and with Peter's successor, and teaching authoritatively on a matter of faith or morals, they are in agreement that a particular judgment is to be held definitively.
>
> *Lumen Gentium*, 25

The Pope can speak infallibly as the head of the college of bishops *when* he speaks as the head of the college of bishops. Modern communications make this much easier to do and verify. For example, before issuing his encyclical called *Evangelium Vitae* ('The Gospel of Life'), in which the rights of the unborn and elderly are defended and upheld, John Paul II consulted extensively around the world.

But can they get it wrong?

Of course they can, and there are plenty of resounding examples in history. It has almost always happened by misunderstanding or by trying to go too far. Most famous is the condemnation of the scientist Galileo in the seventeenth century for insisting that the earth goes round the sun, as opposed to the (then) traditional view that the sun, and everything else, goes round the earth. It seems an utterly daft mistake with hindsight. But hindsight was not available at the time. The Church was trying to defend the authority of scripture, in which various passages talk of the sun standing still, implying solar movement. Nowadays we would give the Bible the respect it truly deserves rather than treating it as a source book for astronomy, but that distinction was not obvious to very many people then. One might even argue that more damage would have been done to the faithful of the time by ditching scriptural authority. That does not excuse the treatment of Galileo, who was condemned and harassed for the rest of his life. A comment of the nineteenth-century writer Cardinal Newman is relevant for all who have, or feel they have, responsibility to teach doctrine to anyone, and all of us who try and understand what they are saying:

> To be a true Catholic one must have a generous loyalty towards
> ecclesiastical authority, and accept what is taught with what is called
> the *pietas fidei* [piety of faith], and only such a tone of mind has a
> claim, and it certainly has a claim, to be met and handled with a wise
> and gentle minimalism. Still, the fact remains, that there has been of
> late years a fierce and intolerant temper abroad, which scorns and
> virtually tramples on the little ones of Christ.
>
> *Letter to the Duke of Norfolk*, 125

The need to bear this in mind is reinforced by some of the absurd
things that have been said by the Church at different times. If you
find the word absurd a little strong, then I must tell you that a
medieval synod once condemned as heretical the notion that 'reading of sacred Scripture is for everyone'. And it does no one any
harm to remember that scorn and trampling and domination have
no justification in the teaching of Christ, whatever they seek to
defend.

In this context we should notice an example in which the Pope
himself has acknowledged mistakes, and sometimes disastrous mistakes, either by popes, by the Church as a whole, or by people who
speak in their name. In March 2000, John Paul II asked pardon of
God for the sins of Christians over the first two millennia. He also
forgave all who had injured Catholics. In his concluding prayer he
prayed for a new Christian future:

> Never again contradictions to charity in the service of truth; never
> again acts against the communion of the Church; never again
> offences against any people; never again recourse to the logic of vio-
> lence; never again discrimination, exclusion, oppression, contempt
> for the poor or the least among us.

This confession, echoed by bishops around the world, including
Germany, Switzerland, Australia and the United States, is a challenge to any of us who hope to be called Christian. It contains a
vision of the Church of the future.

The field in which the Church speaks authoritatively is very
wide, but also quite well defined. A matter has to be 'of faith or
morals'. That is, it has either to be a truth to do with the Gospel, or
else to do with how we live out that Gospel. So, the doctrine of the
Incarnation is to do with faith, and the prohibition of abortion is to

do with morals; though, if you think about it, the Feast of the Annunciation, when we celebrate the conception of the Word made flesh, connects the two themes quite clearly. The Church has no remit to pronounce on the best way to cook an omelette, nor to prescribe a particular remedy for colds. There are many grey areas, however, where the question in doubt bears on the faith. A good example is scientific research into the functioning of the brain. If it starts to deny the spiritual side of humans by saying it is all just neurons firing, then that bears on our belief. Hence the Church spends a lot of time and money trying to keep up to date with the world and its concerns and discoveries.

We are further bound by our tradition. Profound and long reflection led the Church to the definition of the doctrine of the Trinity. We have no right or authority to change that, to declare four Persons or do anything that contradicts the tradition. Other parts of tradition are not so vital, however. Most countries where girls and women are allowed to be servers at Mass or eucharistic ministers have not experienced a collapse of Christian faith. Mistakes arise from giving a particular teaching the wrong weight. This happens all the time, and most people do it, attaching to their favourite aspect of the faith or most congenial devotional practice a special significance. But it becomes malign if a group of people elevate a less important truth or belief to the status of infallible dogma.

Equally absurd, more universal and damaging is to demote a vital part of the faith to something 'not that important'. This is especially easy with moral teaching. Most of us, faced with a sufficiently big temptation, are inclined to stretch points. Somewhere in that process is an internal fib that whatever is in question does not really matter, that the Church's teaching does not really apply in this case and so on. The fib becomes a lie to the extent that we do it on purpose, deliberately setting aside the magisterium, the tradition of the Church, for reasons of convenience. But the motivation can be good; Catholics are often tempted to play down aspects of our faith for the sake of ecumenical harmony.

How to disagree

One thing in particular that the Church cannot command is that you disobey your conscience. There is a very good reason for this:

> In the depths of his conscience man detects a law which he does not
> impose on himself, but which holds him to obedience. Always sum-
> moning him to love good and avoid evil, the voice of conscience can
> when necessary speak to his heart more specifically: 'Do this, shun
> that'. For man has in his heart a law written by God. To obey it is the
> very dignity of man; according to it he will be judged.
>
> Second Vatican Council, *Gaudium et Spes*, 16

If, in conscience, you cannot agree with the Pope or the general magisterium of the Church about any question, then you cannot be condemned. You cannot go to hell for acting or believing according to your conscience. For conscience is the voice of the Holy Spirit, dwelling within you. It cannot err, cannot mislead. What is more, the point of the Gospel is to restore us to the freedom which is ours, so that we can act and be without hindrance according to our nature, the image of God. This is why obeying conscience is the dignity of man: it is what we are made for, to live in the words of God as fish in water.

But, if conscience is to speak divine words, it must be in good order. Suppose you and I are in the same room, looking at the same things. But, for some reason, I see strange and beautiful white and red stars. You just see tables and chairs. Now, I insist that I can see the stars, and you insist that you can't. So I say you are blind or stupid, and you say I am fanciful, making it up or have probably spent too long staring at a computer screen. Who is right? I know reasons why you don't see stars, and you know reasons why I do. What is more, I am absolutely infallible as to what I see, and so are you. I can't fault you on what you see, and you can't fault me; even if you are sure that what I am seeing is not there, you have to accept that I am seeing it. How can we know?

Either there are stars there or there are not. One of us is wrong, one of us has defective vision. But each of us needs something other than us to tell us if we are right. Now, if I am touchy or you are, it may be a difficult and irritating task for whoever it is who has to per-suade me to go and lie down for a while or you to go and get fitted with spectacles. I have to be convinced I am not seeing properly. This means two things. First, someone has to say in an authoritative kind of way, 'You're seeing things. Go and lie down and sleep it off.' Second, I have to be prepared to believe them enough to try it out.

This is the function of Church teaching. It is always to challenge us, in the way the Gospel should always challenge us. The message is unlikely to be welcome if it is truly challenging. It might demand an admission of fault, lack of vision, change of heart or way of living. It might suggest a very different world from the one we find self-evident. But what is at stake is truth. And if what is at stake for me is truth, and not my own cleverness or autonomy or way of life, however precious and apparently good or comfortable, then I am surely sensible enough to entertain what I am told as a point of view. Maybe I even lie down for a while. If I then still see stars, I tell you that you were wrong, and that is fine. But I have heard, tried to understand, looked for a way to fit what you say into my life. That is acting according to conscience, according to human dignity.

For a key part of human dignity, an essential element, is an admission of weakness and of fallibility. Unless that is there, in any case, Jesus can do nothing for you, no matter how right you are. Integrity without a sense of vulnerability is mere pride. Pride is what Christ so desperately wishes to free us from. Someone who is truly human has no difficulty with the fact that his or her inner voice of conscience may well have become obscured by long lazy habit, by lack of nutrition in dialogue with others, or by a basic unwillingness to listen to it. If you know that you can go wrong, then you are also willing to accept help.

So by all means disagree, whether the issue is contraception or how to relate to Lutherans; whether it is the absolute necessity of maniples for a valid celebration of the Eucharist or the world ending when we abandoned the use of Latin. But listen, and always listen. Listen in a particular way. As the very non-Catholic, but occasionally godly, English politician, general and dictator Oliver Cromwell put it: 'I beseech you, in the bowels of Christ, think it possible that you may be mistaken.' In that way, we may be wrong, but we shall not be beyond the help that only Christ can give.

Chapter 13

WALKING CALMLY

I cannot endure festival and solemnity.

Isaiah 1:13

'One thing the Church does really well is to destroy the liturgy.' This judgement is representative of many of the problems experienced in the renewal of Catholic worship after Vatican II. 'Liturgy' is the name we give to the prayer of the Church gathered as a community, usually in a parish for Mass. It comes from a Greek word meaning 'service', worship we offer to God. Many people find the prayer life of their parish deeply satisfying. That is as it should be.

We should also realize, however, that the fissures and tensions within the Church can become painfully visible in the sphere of public liturgy. The tensions and fissures are inevitable, as we saw in chapter 11, and can be taken fruitfully. It is the pain, and how to deal with it, that concerns us here. For a start, one may say that the problem is not a new one. Few problems in the Church are new, and those who like to talk of 'crisis' sometimes lack perspective as well as objectivity. Our story has been one long crisis. It is indeed the crisis of the world, as we all and always face the choice between life and death, between the Cross and self.

One way to understand what the liturgy is about is to think about the Liturgical Year. This tells a story, the story of the life of Jesus.

Advent	Expectation and hope for Christ
Christmas and Epiphany	Birth and revelation of Jesus
Lent	Preparation for Holy Week and Easter

| Holy Week and Easter | The death and resurrection of Jesus |
| Pentecost | The giving of the Holy Spirit |

At another level, the Liturgical Year is also the story of our salvation. It is about the central Christian beliefs in the incarnation, life, death and resurrection of Christ, along with the belief that he will come again in judgement at the end of the world. This mystery is too rich and complex for us to understand, not that this stops us trying, so we re-enact it over the course of a year. During Ordinary Time, the parts of the year not covered by the Christmas and Easter seasons (along with their periods of preparation in Advent and Lent), we celebrate different aspects of the faith, either day to day, or in major feasts such as Christ the King or Trinity Sunday.

In worship together as the Church, we do not just watch or hear about Jesus; we take part in his life and what happened. Hence the more careful we are to take part in the Mass or other services, the more benefit we receive from it. We use different words, gestures and rituals to help us understand God's words and actions in Jesus. At one level, there are such things as vestments of different colours, themed hymns, and various decorations such as the Advent wreath. At a deeper level of significance, we use prayers, readings and special elements such as bread and wine at Mass or water at baptism.

The aim of all this is that through the liturgy, we can actually relive the events we recall. The Mass brings us to the foot of the Cross, there to receive the forgiveness of Christ and to unite ourselves to him as closely as we dare.

At the Last Supper, on the night he was betrayed, our Saviour instituted the eucharistic sacrifice of his Body and Blood. This he did in order to perpetuate the sacrifice of the Cross throughout the ages until he should come again, and so to entrust to his beloved Spouse, the Church, a memorial of his death and resurrection ... Thus recalling the mysteries of the redemption, she opens up to the faithful the riches of her Lord's powers and merits, so that these are in some way made present for all time; the faithful lay hold of them and are filled with saving grace.

Second Vatican Council, *Sacrosanctum Concilium*, 47 and 102

So, what crisis?

Here is a story from safely long ago, the eleventh century, related by David Knowles in his *The Monastic Order in England*. It occurred following the appointment of a certain Thurstan as Abbot of Glastonbury, a large and prosperous Benedictine monastery.

> An *impasse* was finally reached over a question of ceremonies and chant, the abbot insisting on the substitution of the methods of the Dijon school for the Gregorian tradition of which Glastonbury claimed to be inheritor. One day in chapter, after mutual recriminations, Thurstan, losing control of himself, called in his men-at-arms to overawe the monks. The latter fled into the church ... and barricaded themselves in the choir. The men-at-arms ... endeavoured to force their way in and were met with resistance from the monks, who armed themselves with benches and candlesticks; some of their number therefore climbed into the gallery ... and shot down upon the monks who took refuge near and even beneath the altar. The rood was pierced with arrows, which narrowly missed the hanging pyx, and a number of the monks were gravely wounded. Meanwhile, others broke into the choir and attacked them with spears. In all, at least two were killed and a dozen wounded.

So maybe it is not that bad, really. Today, manners are improved, but conceal tensions which are just as real. Here is a sample, taken from two issues of the periodical *Sacred Music*, the official organ of the short-lived Church Music Association of America, whose editors proclaim their determination to

> implement the decrees of the Second Vatican Council, as the council fathers intended ... fighting against those false interpretations that have followed the council, spread by so-called experts in liturgy, wrongly passed off as the 'spirit of the council' and the will of our bishops ... It is against this propaganda, this deliberate violation of the decrees and wishes of the council that we are at war ... at war with those who are disobedient to the Church's directives, and at war with those who promote inferior art.

If that first quotation is merely amusing, this second might cause one to look to the fortifications of the nearest church. The last sentence was written not in the difficult years immediately following the Council, when a certain amount of confusion was only natural, but in 1980 in an article entitled 'The Battle'. It does express a genuine frustration which it is hard to describe without using labels, and rotted labels at that. Within the Church there is a 'conservative' body of opinion, which seeks to preserve what was good in the pre-Vatican II Church, and also a 'liberal' tendency which looks ahead and wants to move on into newer territory. What can easily get lost is that these are both entirely good instincts, and that each is thoroughly necessary to a living body like the Church. A child who is nothing but afraid never leaves the safe haven under the table; a child who is nothing but brave does not stay uninjured for long. The Church is a child growing into God, and, if healthy, looks and is drawn both forwards and backwards.

You have to be very clear, of course, about motivation. Church politics are inevitable, because we are political animals. It is part of our being in the image of God that we relate dynamically. But, as always, that image is threatened by self-interest, fear and guilt. By all means let us campaign, but for what is right and helpful, not just for what we want. Otherwise, things become so easily polarized into those who can only cope with Mass in the old Latin Tridentine rite and those who are all for lay people presiding at the Eucharist. St Benedict recognized this danger when he wrote his monastic *Rule* in the sixth century for a very lively set of monks. He provided, in one of the last chapters, a way of telling if we are doing the right thing for the right reason:

> Just as there is a wicked zeal of bitterness, which separates from God and leads to hell, so there is a good zeal which separates from evil and leads to God and everlasting life. This, then, is the good zeal which monks must foster with fervent love. They should each try to be the first to show respect to the other, supporting with the greatest patience one another's weaknesses of body or behaviour, and earnestly competing in obedience to one another. No one is to pursue what he judges better for himself, but, instead, what he judges better for someone else. To their fellow monks they show the pure love of brothers; to God, loving fear; to their abbot, unfeigned and humble love. Let them prefer nothing whatever to Christ, and may he bring us all together to everlasting life.

Rule, Chapter 72

Violence, be it expressed by the sword or by the mightier pen, does not usually arise of itself in ecclesiastical circles. It is the behaviour of a threatened interest or concern. The monks of Glastonbury were asked to take on board a different way of singing their traditional chants. They perceived behind the 'simple' adjustments a larger issue of a whole new style of abbacy and monasticism. The contributors to *Sacred Music* had witnessed not just the modification of traditional practice, but its almost complete disappearance, especially where music is concerned.

The Second Vatican Council, regardless of the question as to its intention, has resulted in an almost universal transition to a renewed (or new, if you must) vernacular liturgy with a strong emphasis on congregational participation. A generation which has not known anything but the post-conciliar age might be hard put to realize the trauma that this involved. Whole generations of effort at liturgical renewal were suddenly obsolete. It would also be a mistake to suppose that the trauma was limited to liturgists and the theologically literate. Certainly, many are said to have lapsed from the practice of the faith as a result of the Council. But just as telling is the sense that nearly everyone has had at some time of leaving church, after a Mass dignified by music of unsurpassed banality or awfulness, with the feeling that there must be something better than this. Perhaps they may also have shared the feeling of being excluded from participation in the Mass by the very musical forms which were meant to draw us together. 'It's just not my thing,' or, 'How can I sing that!' I know a parish where the readings at the Easter Vigil were cut down to a minimum so as to allow time for the singing of hymns which nobody knew anyway.

On the other hand, the heightened liturgical consciousness that has followed the Council has led to a sensitivity about the use of choirs and trained voices. It has also driven a search for ways in which everyone can take part, from eucharistic ministers giving communion to female altar servers. Most striking and, in my view, beneficial is the change to a language one can understand. But this involves problems if it is taken to mean stamping out the use of Latin, which can be a very dignified language to pray in if you are lucky enough to understand it. One must understand with sympathy those who feel that the Mass is no longer valued as a spectacle which we hear and watch, who feel that they are liturgical orphans. Having been taught by the Council what a beautiful object the liturgy is, and reluctant to conceal it again under its former rich coverings, we clothe it instead with rags or with material randomly gathered.

A way forward

Notice how difficult it is to avoid violent language! After such a gloomy beginning it might improve morale to hear the exasperation of St Pius X, faced in 1903, at the beginning of his pontificate, with a crisis in church music that places our own in perspective.

> It is vain to hope for blessings from Heaven if our worship of the Most High, rather than ascending with an odour of sweetness, again puts into Our Lord's hands the scourges with which the unworthy profaners were once driven out of the temple by the Divine Redeemer.
>
> *Tra le sollecitudini*, Preface

Even if we allow for irony and hyperbole, this is strong language. The pope believes that if our worship is not up to scratch we will be driven away by God, just as Jesus expelled the money-changers. The Church is to be a house of prayer, not of liturgical statements. The issue is not whether *you* like it, but whether *God* likes it; not how liturgy *feels*, but what it *is*.

There is a temptation on all parts of the political spectrum to forget what communal prayer is about. It is about praying. It is about praying together. It involves recognizing that liturgy is about God, not about our own self-expression. This is important to realize because it applies to those who cannot live without Latin just as much as to those who feel they have to be slain by the Spirit every Sunday. We are not just celebrating our faith, we are receiving from God.

It does matter what you do, on two levels. First, and fundamentally, the worship of the Church is all about the movement from God to us in Christ for our salvation. Liturgy reflects the fact that we are helpless, and quite probably seasick, in a little boat until Jesus comes to rescue us by his presence. The initiative is all his, in Incarnation, Cross and Resurrection, and it is this that he wants to share with us. We are given the liturgy to be our way of coming into contact with God and the grace he offers. This *given* aspect is reflected in the liturgical books: missals, lectionaries and the like.

Our choice of what we do is restricted by the Church: purple, not yellow, is the colour for Advent; we use this prayer, not that one, on the third Sunday in Ordinary Time. We should do what is laid down not just because a lot of clever people have spent nearly two thousand years constructing the rules so that we cover in a year the whole of revelation, but because submitting to what is given is our only hope of salvation. You can either stay in the boat, or you can walk on the water; if you can walk on the water, fine and lucky you.

But I can't. And because I know I can't, I am inclined to restrain my instinct to try and remodel the boat so that it suits me better. It might fall apart in the process, and there probably would not be room for any of you in it, especially if you continue to disagree with my sincerely held convictions about the best way to hold an oar. Jesus was under few illusions about our tendencies to independence. He gives us an incentive to stick together with what we have:

> I tell you solemnly once again, if two of you on earth agree to ask anything at all, it will be granted to you by my Father in heaven. For where two or three meet in my name, I shall be there with them.
>
> Matthew 18:19–20

There is something very powerful about the witness of a group of people praying together. Our common prayer is our most effective means of evangelizing. We look like and *are* the Body of Christ, his presence in the world. But Jesus underwrites the effort required with a deeper promise. He will be with us. It is worth dwelling on what is implied if two or three meet together in Jesus' name, the level of unity which is required. In fact, if you think about what we are really like, it is nothing short of a miracle in itself. By putting up with each other in contact with God (and it would surely be easier on your own) we find that the deepest wound in our human nature, our alienation from God, is healed in the healing of our alienation from each other. Saying prayers together is, at the least, showing willing, which is all the Father needs in order to give us his Son and fill us with his Spirit.

In other words, worship together is tolerant by its very nature. The title of this chapter comes from one of my brethren who tends to find the complexities of monastic liturgy rather challenging. He defines liturgy as 'walking calmly in the wrong direction'. Any form of worship which seeks to dominate or write off any other form of worship within the Church is not liturgical prayer, and we need to beware being driven from the Temple; Christ will not be with us if we are not with each other. The forms of words which we are given in the tradition of the Church make it easy to be together in prayer; why not use them? The books are surprisingly rich in what they provide, and they are getting richer as the renewal and revision of rites continues.

Clergy and laity alike need to be encouraged to explore them. I will give one example: visiting the sick. It is still fairly common for priests or parish sisters to visit the sick and dying, mutter an 'Our Father' and a 'Jesus, Mary and Joseph' and then a 'Thanks, I'd love some tea'. Nothing wrong with that at all, but there is more available, which can enrich what we already do. The new – though not that new – book called *Pastoral Care of the Sick* contains several short, untaxing, simple and rather beautiful rites for use with people who are gravely ill: a short reading, a prayer and a blessing. Anyone can use them, not just clergy, and anyone can benefit if they are used.

Keeping calm

The view becomes clouded, however, because we all get so anxious and dogmatic about liturgical matters. You hear people going on about how everyone must be made to 'take part'. This flies in the face of a venerable tradition among, for example, English Catholics of leaving the front ten or so rows empty and sitting at the back of the church, or even thronging the porch. Priests and parish worthies feel such failures if they cannot persuade such people to sit at the front, take up the gifts, read readings and bellow with enthusiasm hymns and songs consisting of theologically correct and expressive lyrics set to 'accessible' tunes.

On the other hand, you hear people saying that what went wrong was that the Church cut itself off from its heritage in abandoning the old Latin Mass, that congregations have drained away because we have abandoned the sense of awe and majesty of God. There is something in this. An accessible God has less power to frighten, and a bland, unchallenging liturgy does not always raise anything more than one's eyes to heaven. However, you can, and people do, take it too far if you say that lots of incense, plainchant and Latin is the 'only' way. It may be the only way for you, which is a bit of a shame; but there are other people and other ways. While it is true that the Council did not anticipate a rapid and universal movement away from Latin and into lay participation, it certainly did permit it. We have no authority to deny people the right to pray as they can, and no warrant to say that our way is better.

Another approach has been to open the liturgy to feelings and enthusiasm, and this characterizes the Charismatic Renewal. We are to look for the energy of the Holy Spirit, and seek to encourage its manifestations, whether these be spontaneous revelations or speaking in tongues. Music tends to be upbeat, rhythmic and with a strong emphasis on joy and empowerment. Worship in this way is very often uplifting, encouraging and a marvellous experience of growth in trust and love of God.

Some people, however, just can't stand that form of worship. There is no reason why they should. Sometimes charismatics can talk as though nobody else in the Church believes in the Holy Spirit. They can imply that unless one has experience of vivid conversion, one is lacking something critical. Once again, though, people differ, and it is good that they do. Our Church is a rich community that can afford to give room to all types of temperament, and hence all kinds of ways of praying. Formal liturgy gives us the roof under which we shelter; it keeps us together and allows us to stay apart.

And if we have the patience to put up with it, something very special happens. For we come to pray not as ourselves but as the whole community of believers, not as a bunch of people, but as the Body of Christ. We celebrate then the mystery of our salvation, but also enact that mystery, make it present. It is a fact of our life that this involves Cross as much as Resurrection, and a fact about God that the more we will give way to others, the more he will bless our own prayer.

The Church is essentially both human and divine, visible, but endowed with invisible realities, zealous in action and dedicated to contemplation, present in the world, but as a pilgrim, so constituted that the human is directed toward the divine, and this present world to that city yet to come, the object of our quest.

The liturgy daily builds up those who are in the Church, making of them a holy temple of the Lord, a dwelling place for God in the Spirit, to the mature measure of the fullness of Christ. At the same time it marvellously increases their power to preach Christ and thus show forth the Church, a sign lifted up among the nations, to those who are outside, a sign under which the scattered children of God may be gathered together until there is one fold and one shepherd.

Second Vatican Council, *Sacrosanctum Concilium*, 2

Chapter 14

LOST FOR EVER?

I shall look for the lost one and make the weak strong.

Ezekiel 34:16

Let us now turn to a very difficult subject – those lapsed from Catholicism. To do so, we will return to my first acquaintance on the train journey of enquirers. He was an old man with two sons, and was genuinely concerned for their welfare, since both had lapsed from the practice of the faith in which he had brought them up. Many people can relate to this situation, and their anxiety can have a number of levels. A mother can easily feel that she has some-how failed as a parent, that there was something not passed on which should have been. For some people, there is a deep alarm that their children are lost, damned, unless they can be brought back to regular Mass attendance.

The crisis can break when grandchildren appear: 'They are not even married, Father.' Attempts by grandparents to intervene, to 'at least have her christened, darling', to provide generous support for Catholic education, to get the little ones aside for a 'talk' about the meaning of life, can very easily come to nothing. Everybody ends up aggrieved and the rifts can take years to heal, if they ever do. At worst, parents can drive their offspring even further from Catholic practice by sheer force of example if they come across as bigoted, or simply by the usual counter-productive effects of nagging. So, what can they do?

The first step might be to try and understand what 'lapsed' Catholics are rejecting. One can say with some confidence that it is very unlikely that anyone is out to reject God, or trample on any crucifixes; though, as I say, it is quite possible to drive them to that. It is important to understand what is actually being said. A certain reaction to an over religious childhood, or to a sense of having been 'forced to go to Church', especially at a time before about three in the afternoon, is frequent and understandable and sometimes articulated even as atheism. A revulsion at the evil in the world, or the darker side of Christians, is almost to be approved, provided one realizes that this is not the end of the story but a beginning of a new growth in faith, often unconscious and frequently slow. The second might be to clarify what one actually wants for them – is it merely a social conformity, or are we alarmed when a son or daughter suddenly starts to think for themselves? It should be said in passing that Catholicism is as well suited to empty, lukewarm conformity as any other habitual activity: be honest about your own religion.

Maybe those two steps seem a little harsh. After all, *they* are the ones who have lapsed, not you. I put it this way partly because it is important to be clear, but also because I would hope to win the sympathetic audience of non-practising Catholics. Are they sure what they are rejecting, and why? Are they actually rejecting anything? Is it not better for someone to act according to their beliefs, which includes being true to the lack of them? The label 'lapsed' may often be too harsh. One major concern is that people see too many stark black and white choices: do/think this, or be Catholic. For example, using contraceptives, living unmarried with a partner, thinking that no good God could permit all the evil in the world, having been desperately hurt by a priest, never praying, being a bad husband, hating your mother, cheating the welfare state, or whatever. You can do all these and be Catholic; maybe not a very good Catholic, but who is? Let us be sinners. It is better than being Pharisees.

If you have read the first six or so chapters of this book, and accepted the contract in the introduction, then we already share the great secret: God is interested in saving people, not judging them. After all, he can safely leave the judging to us; we are much better at it, having had more practice. I hear a crusty voice saying, 'But what about the Last Judgement?' Okay, let's talk about the Last Judgement, that charter of crustiness. You probably know the story, but it merits repetition, because it is so easily misunderstood.

When the Son of Man comes in his glory, escorted by all the angels, then he will take his seat on his throne of glory. All the nations will be assembled before him and he will separate men one from another as the shepherd separates sheep from goats. He will place the sheep on his right hand and the goats on his left. Then the king will say to those on his right hand, 'Come, you whom my Father has blessed, take for your heritage the kingdom prepared for you since the foundation of the world. For I was hungry and you gave me food; I was thirsty and you gave me drink; I was a stranger and you made me welcome; naked and you clothed me, sick and you visited me, in prison and you came to see me.' Then the virtuous will say to him in reply, 'Lord, when did we see you a stranger and make you welcome ... sick or in prison and go to see you?' And the King will answer, 'I tell you solemnly, in so far as you did this to one of the least of these brothers of mine, you did it to me.'

Matthew 25:31–46

The wicked goats then have a mirror-image conversation with Christ and are led off to eternal punishment. What can we gather from this parable? There is indeed judgement, and a judgement to fear. We really can blow it. But we knew this already, indeed we do not need the Gospel to tell us that; it is a default setting to think that! Looking at the judgement more closely, there is an obvious pattern, however. It is those who have shown mercy, in its older sense of practical pity, who are judged to be virtuous. Those who denied mercy are denied mercy.

So far, this is a positive version of the standard revenge eye-for-eye ethic that is one of the main curses of our fallen knowledge of good and evil. But behind it is a question of how we look at people: do we see Christ in them? Then is the question asked as to whether we act like Christ towards them. As one would expect, faith precedes works, and works presuppose faith. This is important because the Judgement is not about laws and rules; not primarily. It is, in a final analysis, because it is right to visit the sick, feed the hungry, and so on. But if you can take a moment off your busy programme of following these precepts to the full, note that the Judgement is actually about people, first of all, and bringing Christ to them.

Living by the law

This should not be too surprising, since we know by now that God is quite interested in people, and will do almost anything to get them back to his love. We are expected at least to try to have the same perspective, if we really cannot refrain from judging. Let's take a law:

> The Sunday Eucharist is the foundation and confirmation of all Christian practice. For this reason the faithful are obliged to participate in the Eucharist on days of obligation, unless excused for a serious reason (for example, illness, the care of infants) or dispensed by their own pastor. Those who deliberately fail in this obligation commit a grave sin.
>
> *Catechism of the Catholic Church*, 2181

That is pretty clear. 'So, everyone who fails to go to Mass every Sunday is in mortal sin.' Well, maybe it is not that clear. Any church rule has a reason behind it, and usually, especially in the new *Code of Canon Law*, this reason is made explicit, and we are expected to use our heads a bit. The reason here is a fairly self-evident one; the weekly Mass is the foundation and confirmation of our Christian practice. Deliberately to deny this importance is to be in grave sin.

I should warn you that I am now about to come up with what could be called a piece of typical liberal nonsense. But it seems obvious that if you are not a practising Christian, there is no practice to have a foundation or confirmation. Sinful denial is about shutting your eyes to what you know to be true. Some things are more clearly true than others. We all know it is wrong to cut your husband's head off if he sings in the bath, and none of us do that, unless pushed beyond reason. But someone who does not find or think the Mass to be central to their life is not denying anything, just disbelieving. If your practice has no foundation because you have no practice, you cannot be blamed for failing to confirm a foundation that is not there. You cannot reject God without meaning to, he will not let you.

Just to make it clear, the law cited applies to a practising Catholic, who knows all about the Mass, believes in it, but decides to play golf instead. That is mortal sin, other things being equal. It is indeed a harsh law, and it applies to those of us who think of ourselves as good Catholics. To go against your conscience on such a matter is to play dice (if not golf) with the devil. With regard to lapsed Catholics, the more relevant question of sin is concerned with we who judge them, and those who might have driven them away.

I should warn you now that I am going to say something that could be called rather conservative. All baptized Catholics should attend the Mass on Sunday and other holy days of obligation. It is a sign of a serious disorder that any of them should not. The next paragraph in the *Catechism* tells us why.

> Participation in the communal celebration of the Sunday Eucharist is a testimony of belonging and of being faithful to Christ and to his Church. The faithful give witness by this to their communion in faith and charity. Together they testify to God's holiness and their hope of salvation. They strengthen one another under the guidance of the Holy Spirit.
>
> *Catechism of the Catholic Church*, 2182

That is what lapsed Catholics are deprived of. It is why they have lapsed, because they have been deprived of communion in faith or charity, have lost their hope of salvation. The communal Eucharist is no longer an expression of those things for them. If we want to judge them to help them, we have to see them as distinct persons, each with different reasons and difficulties. The disorder of which I speak is much deeper than not toeing a line. Crusty types need to realize that it is far worse than they thought.

Living

Quite often, the disorder does not lie in the people concerned. A young family, with all the heavy distractions of trying to live and stay together in a hostile city environment, may have too much to contend with day to day to be able to keep one of those days holy. A young student, meeting new ideas for the first time, may well be persuaded out of behaving 'like a machine' and deluded into 'thinking for himself'. Another, pressed by family custom or school rules into a piety that has become empty, may naturally seek fresh air on leaving home; he or she has not believed for years. My own view is that the Father is probably delighted if that family survives and the boy or girl ceases to behave like a machine, and the other one starts at last to live by his own principles and conscience rather than his parents' practice, but that is another issue.

One has to be realistic, too, about how things are today. Long ago, say in the 1950s, everything was very straightforward. All kinds of things were clear, from going to church on Sunday to politics, sex and public finances. You could tell where people were from by their accent and, in England, how much money they had. Society was ordered, postmen saluted and there was honey for tea and all that. What is like that now? How many 'traditional' values and practices are accepted without question? Does anyone think any more that it is a self-evidently good use of a young life to die for one's country? Nothing is fixed, solid, predictable, it has all gone post-modern. It would be odd indeed if young people's religious expression had remained fixed, predictable.

It is quite possible that not going to Mass *is* an expression of faith. That is not quite as mad as it sounds. Suppose a boy or girl has a strong instinct for truth, and for trying to do the right thing. Maybe they are confused and mixed up, but maybe they also have a yearning for a bit of peace and meaning. Perhaps they are charitable, after their way, and even do something to help those in need. A sheep, or a goat? Then present them with a drab worshipping community that has turned its back on the lapsed, that is religiously secure, whose God is allowed to give them no more than a superficial sense of holiness and a profound sense of respectability. Goats, or sheep? Perhaps the young person has a sense of identity, of being uniquely themselves, free. Then present them with an institution which demands conformity, that tells them they have failed before they began. What would they have to sacrifice to go to church, how much integrity? There is a danger that we are simply insisting that people walk on water, when Christ is already right next to them.

Even if you will not concede that it is sometimes right to blame society or us, perhaps I can console you with a more solid truth. Christian life is just that, a Christian lifetime. Even monuments of Catholic practice only express real, honest religion in times of need. That is, after all, our working definition of religion, the acknowledgement of need. It is not, therefore, necessarily a cause for surprise or papal interdict if people, at different times of life, drift in and out of religion. We forget Jesus if we do not need him, or rather, if we forget that we do need him. Lapsed Catholics are maybe a bit more honest, realistic, in their practice of what is actually the irreligion of us all. If you disagree, you are missing something about yourself and about God.

It perhaps sounds as though I am saying there is no value or virtue to practising the faith. God forgives us, takes us as we are. If Jane and Pete, who never go to Mass any more, are not lost, why should I bother going? The answer is simply that *you* do understand and believe in the Mass, in what it is. As we saw above, this consciousness gives, of itself, an obligation; otherwise, we live a lie. But let us remember what the Mass is about. It tells us of the Word made flesh, giving himself to us for our salvation. It also *is* the Word made flesh, giving himself to us for our salvation. He does this out of his love for us, not because we have gone there. The grace of Christ is gift, not reward. This, then, is our witness, it is to the forgiveness of God for all who stray. We have seen that truth, and desire to show it to others. If this is what grounds our churchgoing, then our testimony will be authentic, it will speak with the full force of the Word to hearts that yearn for him whom they do not know.

In all respects, the Father speaks in *our* language, in our life. After all, he wants us to understand him, to hear his voice. Once we have heard, he can help us, and help us he will. We have seen how he will not force, he will not act without our consent, and this is the last and most important point for parents worried about their apparently faithless offspring. Maybe, as I have suggested, they do believe. Maybe they do not. But *you* do. They do not seek the grace of God in the sacraments. But *you* do. Each time you are at Mass you can offer them with yourself, and that will be enough. It is as real as when you spoke the baptismal vows for them. By your consent, your patient and loving witness to God's patient love, he will find ways to draw his children to himself. But the ways are his, not yours; and not theirs either. 'Then the virtuous will say to him in reply, "Lord, when did we see you a stranger and make you welcome ... sick or in prison and go to see you?" And the King will answer, "I tell you solemnly, in so far as you did this to one of the least of these brothers of mine, you did it to me."'

The last word can go to St Augustine, one of the most spectacularly wayward lapsed Catholics in the Church's history, who, before he became a bishop and one of the Church's greatest thinkers, dabbled in all kinds of superstitions and wayward lusts. He came back, because his mother never gave up her prayer for him. Her witness got through, when he realized that her God knew more about his problems and needs than he did himself. Here is what he said to the Father, looking back. It is a word of hope for those of us, too, who do not have the courage to lapse.

Late have I loved you, O Beauty so ancient and so new; late have I loved you! For you were within me, and I outside; and I sought you outside and in my unloveliness fell upon those lovely things which you have made. You were with me, and I was not with you ... You called and cried to me, and broke open my deafness ... You touched me, and I have burned for your peace.

Confessions, 10.27

Chapter 15

OUT OF COMMUNION

The tongue of stammerers will speak clearly.

Isaiah 32:4

After all that has been said about sacraments as our link with Christ, we have to remember that many Catholics are barred from receiving them. On the whole, these are good people, good Catholics, except in one thing. The two largest groups of them are remarried divorcees and practising homosexuals. In this chapter, I want to leave aside the ethical issues of these situations. We will look at these in a later chapter and concentrate here on a specific problem: that there are rules in the Church which ban people from communion and from confession and thus, by extension, from the rest of the sacraments. For now, I want to think about how people might cope with being outcasts from their own Church, and how those who are not outcast should consider them.

We may as well take the bleakest approach to begin with. The Gospels contain much about the forgiveness of sin. But there is also some very unwelcome, uncompromising language from Jesus about faults and the need for correction.

> If your brother does something wrong, go and have it out with him alone, between your two selves. If he listens to you, you have won back your brother. If he does not listen, take one or two others along with you: the evidence of two or three witnesses is required to sustain any charge. But if he refuses to listen to these, report it to the community; and if he refuses to listen to the community, treat him like a pagan or a tax collector.

Matthew 18:15–20

There it is, an insistence that it is possible for a Christian to put him or her self beyond the limits of community. Jesus gives licence for someone to be expelled. Behind this harsh judgement lies an important insight, however. Even a private fault or quarrel can take on a communal aspect. In the light of what we have seen in previous chapters, this is not surprising, even if it needs emphasis. Even a small lack of love between two people on a tiny issue can spread like a virus – computer or other – across the whole world. A hits B, who hits C, who ... Great wars are built up of many smaller hates and conflicts. The Christian contrast is of a society of forgiveness, where we turn the other cheek in trying to show to each other the love that God has shown to us in Christ.

Do the words of Jesus just quoted imply that there is a time, a point in the breakdown of a relationship, when we can stop putting up with offences, can rest from forgiving, and simply expel? After all, he also tells us that what we bind on earth is considered bound in heaven. Undoubtedly this permission to cast someone out has been used in the past, and is used today. There is even less doubt that the power has been misused. For I do not think Jesus means that we can chuck out the rebel when we can no longer cope. If he did mean this, then the measure of the Church's love is the extent to which we can humanly cope. But that is wrong. The love in the Church is the love of the Trinity, the Holy Spirit, which has no measure. If we can no longer take the bad behaviour, that is a fact about *our* limits, how much can be coped with, not about how much bad behaviour *should* be tolerated.

'Well, I know plenty of people who take no notice of what I say!' That is beside the point. Jesus has in mind someone who will not listen to anything or anybody. Not a private word, not a few well-meant interventions, not the whole community of believers can persuade the offender that he or she has done wrong and should reform or make amends. There is a question of truth here. From one side, that of the person who will not listen, there is no problem. If there is a problem, 'it is with these do-gooding people who keep pestering and nagging about nothing. I have done nothing wrong, or I did it for good reasons, or they do just as bad or worse, or he started it so it is his fault, or it's a private matter to me, none of anybody else's business.'

In such a case, the action recommended by Jesus is not a punishment, or a sentence, or even really an action of the community.

It is a declaration of what is the case, that the wrong-doer has gone out of orbit. As such, this is not necessarily an aggressive move. In the *Rule* of St Benedict, written for the fairly uncouth circumstances of a sixth-century monastery, there is provision for a form of excommunication. This is not the same as formal ecclesiastical excommunication, but an internal, community matter. A bad monk can be banned from community prayer and meals; he has to pray and eat alone. A very, very bad monk can be kicked out of the monastery, but only after a long period of excommunication in which he has a chance to reflect. The point of excommunication in the Rule is not to drive the monk away, but to make clear to him how far he has already taken himself from the community by the paths of behaviour he has chosen, and the attitudes of thought and feeling that lie behind his actions. The abbot is to send him sensible and kind monks to counsel him and keep him from despair. As soon as the monk accepts the truth that he has wandered far away, he is welcomed back into the communal life of repentance.

I mention the monastic case, because it illustrates very well what Jesus has in mind here. He is putting forward suggestions about how to bring someone back into the love of the community, not stages of a disciplinary process aimed towards expulsion. Formal excommunication is a rare event; you have to push the boat out in a big way. Offences include apostasy, heresy and schism, attempting to say Mass or to absolve when not a priest, telling people what someone has said in confession, hitting the Pope, sacrilegious use of consecrated hosts and procuring an abortion. It is also easily undone, usually by the bishop, on repentance by those involved. In danger of death, any priest can absolve. The aim of a formal sentence is to bring people back, by first making them aware of how far away they have gone.

It is vital to get this the right way round, and especially vital if we will admit that the Church as a whole has got this wrong from time to time, often thereby causing great suffering. The traditional scapegoat here is the Inquisition. But this is a scapegoat, though admittedly a worthy candidate for that honour. Another scapegoat is 'the Church', another is the hierarchy, another is the Pope, or the popes; and the most popular scapegoat at the moment is the Curia, the Vatican, or the Congregation for the Doctrine of the Faith.

These are not free of guilt. We will come back to the problems of the human Church as it faces its divine vocation in the next chapter. For present purposes, I want to insist that all of them, even if they are in truth as black as black, are still only scapegoats. The Church, or any one part of it, only condemns people because it is made up of people who condemn other people. Yes, I mean me, and more especially I mean you. I blame you, it's all your fault. And you might blame me. Do you see what I mean? The origin of Christian intolerance is in the intolerance of Christians; anything that excoriates or excommunicates a fellow believer. It is so easy. There are so many levels at which one can cast doubt on another's motivation, faith, or piety. Excommunication should not happen among the people of God. It does happen because we are not what we should be in the love of God. Let those who are themselves without sin in this respect cast the first stone at the Church.

The same principles apply when we come to think about people who are barred from receiving communion. These are not excommunicated. Their case is that they are in a state of sin, sufficiently serious to be called mortal. Anyone in mortal sin should not receive communion until they have confessed and received absolution, or at least formed the full intention of doing so. Some people cannot be absolved, however, because absolution is dependent on contrition. The grace of the sacrament of Reconciliation cannot touch someone who is not sorry for their sins and has no intention of trying to avoid them in future. That goes for all of us. But here is the bind. Two groups of people in particular are touched by it, as mentioned before: remarried divorcees, whose previous marriage has not been annulled, and practising homosexuals. In the phrase of the *Code of Canon Law*, these 'obstinately persist in manifest grave sin' (Canon 915).

The injustice lies in the word 'manifest'. Two women are next to each other in church one Sunday. Mary was granted a civil divorce, after her husband of twenty years left her for someone he had met on business. She lived alone for nine years, trying to rebuild her life. Last year she met John, also divorced, at her golf club. They shared stories and fell in love, and are now married in civil law. She goes to Mass every Sunday, and on weekdays, when the weather is too bad for golf. John has no fixed religious beliefs, but happily drives her to church and waits outside. Nearly sixty, she takes part in parish activities and is always first to welcome newcomers. But she cannot receive communion. Her neighbour, Jo, has just left her place to go up to the sanctuary because she is a eucharistic minister. Jo is a bit of a politician, and irons all the altar cloths out of spite, so that none of the other women get their hands on them. She attends to Father's secretarial needs, and is the terror of the small party which cleans the church on Tuesdays. In her heart she despises Mary, and gets a secret thrill out of going up to give communion from sitting near her, because she knows it hurts.

Which of the two is in sin? Which in grave sin? Which in manifest grave sin? We give the likes of Jo the benefit of the doubt. We give ourselves the benefit of the doubt. We even thank God that we are not like those who are excluded from the free gift of life, the God who comes to call sinners. This all seems wrong. Nobody should receive communion, we are none of us worthy. Then how can we suppose that the word of healing is spoken only to some and not to others? There are worse things than rebuilding your life in its last years, than finding a new 'father' for your children after their own has walked out. I could find worse things in my own heart if I dared to look.

Nobody is entitled to say anything on this issue unless they can know what it is to be rejected. The full force of the uncomfortable procedure put forward by Jesus in the extract above is found in its last prescription. Suppose someone really is beyond the pale, has gone too far, will not listen, persists in their manifest state of grave sin. Then, 'if he refuses to listen to the community, treat him like a pagan or a tax collector'. This is not what it seems. How did Jesus treat pagans? How did he treat tax collectors? There was a Roman centurion, the representative of an oppressive foreign and pagan power, of whom Jesus said, 'not even in all Israel have I found such faith'. There was a tax collector to whom he said, 'Follow me,' and another who heard him say, 'Zacchaeus, make haste and come down, for I must stay with you today.' If one who is 'out of communion' does not hear from you, a sacramentally practising Christian, a message like that, then you do not speak in Christ's name, do not think in his way. You may be further from him than they are. Jesus was stigmatized by the chatteringly righteous religious people of his day as one who 'welcomes sinners and eats with them'.

If you are barred from the sacraments and do not hear that message from your fellow Christians, do not judge them; at least, try not to. Do not doubt that the message of Christ given to Zacchaeus and Matthew and Paul and St Augustine and so on is also for you.

But I cannot deny a contradiction between that truth and the practice of the Church. Without judgement, how can we understand this?

First, let us remember that sacraments are not exclusive channels, in the sense that in them and in them only is the grace of God to be found. The sacraments are more like guarantees; grace *is* there. People need sacraments because we need such assurances that we can be and are in communion with Christ in love. Sacraments are ways in which God deals with our *lack* of faith. 'Yes,' he says, 'I am here.' This is not to devalue sacraments, because the expression and admission of need on that level of doubt and faith is essential to the action of grace. So sacraments are necessary, if only because they humble us by putting things in words of one syllable. We believe and do not believe, and so God meets us where we are. The more purple the language we use of sacraments, the more we describe the depth of our need.

But that means that he is not confined by his guarantee. If you buy a car, it might have a two- or five-year warranty in which the maker promises that it will proceed in predictable directions at desired times and not fall to pieces at 60 mph and stop. If it fails to meet the stated performance, the thing is put right at the manufacturer's expense. But only a very odd person indeed would rejoice if the fenders rusted off or the engine seized up for no reason on the day after the warranty expired. Most people would hope that the car would still function in recognizably car-like ways for some time afterwards. The guarantee is not a statement that the car will only work for two years or five.

If we give God credit for being at least as well intentioned and honest, not to say intelligent, as the average car dealer, then we can say that he gives us his grace in lots of ways. But what is this grace? What do we mean by communion? In the sacraments we are after one thing and one thing alone, which is contact with the risen Christ. There are other points of contact. Some of them are perhaps in some senses points of fuller contact even than the sacraments. Let us think of Jo and Mary at Mass on Sunday, or on Tuesday if it is raining. There are two ways of looking at the question of communion. We can ask, 'Which of them is closer to Christ?' I have suggested several times in this and previous chapters that this is not a very wise question. If it has an answer, we are not likely to be able to bear the responsibility of having asked it; we are taken too close to being the Pharisee. There is a second question, though: 'To which of them is Christ closest?' Again, this is not a simple question, but it is less dangerous. I have no intention of answering it even in this simple hypothetical case, let alone a real and complex human situation. But some answers are illuminating. One of these is suggested by St Paul, talking of Jesus and his Incarnation:

> For our sake, God made the sinless one into sin, so that in him we might become the goodness of God.
>
> 1 Corinthians 5:21

Where is Jesus, then? I dare not take this further than to say that there are means of communion very different from the tidy and unthreatening sacraments, distorted as they can be by our sinful pride. The risen Christ is also Christ the crucified criminal. Yes, he was unjustly condemned; but who in your church (or out of your church) can *you* condemn with justice? No human exclusions from grace are just; they are no more than reflections of our wrecked capacity to relate and forgive. We cannot be too sure, then, of where he is today in our worship. Maybe Jo goes up to receive Christ, and leaves him sitting in the pew, right next to Mary. Maybe Mary can be in communion with her Lord. The experience may not be too far from that of St Paul himself, who became, with his companions, so close to Jesus that they were

> taken for imposters while we are genuine; obscure yet famous; said to be dying and here we are alive; rumoured to be executed before we are sentenced; thought most miserable and yet we are always rejoicing; taken for paupers though we make others rich; for people having nothing though we have everything.
>
> 1 Corinthians 6:10

Chapter 16

OTHER SHEEP

Catch the little foxes for us that make havoc of the vineyard.

Song of Songs 2:15

One of the saddest happenings in life is when a family becomes divided into factions. Maybe one sister has always failed to get on with another, and once they are adults and have families of their own, the feud begins in earnest. There are no visits, no calls. Sometimes people pretend the others do not exist, and only acknowledge that they do in an exchange of Christmas cards that makes the snow outside seem warm.

The rift can happen for lots of reasons in many different ways. A common pattern is for a time of stress, such as the long-term illness or death of a parent, to uncover tensions that already exist. One side may accuse the other of 'not looking after him properly' or claim that 'she really wants to be with us' or go into a home or whatever. The terrible part is that it is all so automatic. Perfectly nice and reasonable people find themselves saying things they do not want to mean, and doing things they never wished to do, trapped into a spiral of growing resentment.

An example at the back of my mind is a story told me by a friend about a long and deep row in his family. Nobody can remember its cause, but it was something to do with my friend's grandfather marrying a Catholic and himself converting. It went on and on, with mutual failures to attend baptisms – the non-Catholics in case they got turned into green frogs by papist magic, and the Catholics because they would have no part with unbelief – and briefest possible encounters at weddings or funerals. Perhaps you are not far from knowing of, or being in, a situation as absurd yourself. Anyway, the grandchildren, or some of them, decided once they were grown up that enough was enough. After months of persuasion, tears, blackmail, bullying and bribery, they managed to arrange for a reconciliation; there was going to be a buffet supper at the non-Catholic home. Much effort went into the meal, formally laying out a long table and so on. All the guests had arrived, and they went through into the dining room and the Catholic grandparents stormed out because it was a beef casserole and this was a Friday.

How stupid! Each side is to blame: the Catholics for not realizing that the others might have simply forgotten about a regulation that is no longer in force anyway (we are meant to take on a small penance or special prayer on Friday in commemoration of the Crucifixion, but what is now up to us) rather than being out to get them, the non-Catholics for being thoughtless. The situation is now beyond retrieval this side of the grave. I mention this example because it shows well how easily enmity can snowball until nothing can be done about it, even if people want to. Past a certain stage, anything that is said or done is suspect as a hidden insult, or as a point being made, or as insincere because they want to inherit the grandfather clock. At best, one patches up a surface peace under which the fires smoulder. Yet, anyone who has experienced the genuine reconciliation that can happen across generations and the most appalling misunderstandings or even abuse, cannot but wish it for all.

Is it correct to assume that our natural state is to be at peace with each other? Here is where the matter bears on Church unity and ecumenism. One should ask, realistically, what kind of standard we should aim at. Jesus himself seems to have had a fairly clear idea about this in his last prayer to the Father before his death:

> Holy Father, keep those you have given me true to your name, so that they may be one like us ... I pray not only for these, but for those who through their words will believe in me. May they all be one. Father, may they be one in us, as you are in me and I am in you, so that the world may believe that it was you who sent me. I have given them the glory you gave to me, that they may be one as we are one.
>
> John 17:11, 21–2

History seems to have decided very differently. The Church has been divided from its beginnings over the most important questions. One apostle, St John, was at the foot of the Cross, while the rest were elsewhere in fear and hiding; that was the first and in some ways the decisive schism. Yet they were reconciled. I have mentioned in chapter 12 the tension over non-Jewish converts that split the early Church. It was comparatively harmless, compared to the question of the human and divine natures of Christ which was settled by gang warfare on the streets of fourth- and fifth-century Alexandria. In 1053 Eastern and Western Christianity finally split over the wording of the Creed, though the schism had been opening for several hundred years over issues of jurisdiction and mission territory. Then, the Protestant Reformation of the sixteenth century shattered the Christian community into what eventually became hundreds of fragments, most of them militantly convinced of their own right and the eternal damnation of the others. Wars and persecutions that would have made a Roman emperor blush for shame were launched between fellow baptized disciples of the Christ who prayed that they might be one, and who sacrificed himself to bring us peace.

There is no doubt what Jesus intends. His followers are to be united. But not just united in the sense of agreeing with each other, or all doing the same things. That is rather a superficial kind of unity; it is found in model railway clubs and marine battalions. Jesus is talking about a unity which we cannot really imagine, the unity of the three Persons of the Trinity. You and I are to become one as Christ is one with his Father and the Holy Spirit. There is no more fundamental oneness than that, even if we cannot say much about it.

One thing that can be said, though, is that it is a union of Persons. The Father is not the Son, nor is he the Holy Spirit. And so on. Each is God, but each is distinct. The Persons are not different aspects of God, different ways of talking about the same thing (the Church split over that one quite spectacularly in the second century) but different 'things' themselves. Yet there is only one God. It is a matter of taste how you want to boggle your mind; you can either try and work out how three distinct Persons that are God add up to one God, or how the undivided Godhead can be in three distinct Persons. But the answer to both is very simple, and we find it in ourselves. If you remember, back in chapter 4, we saw in the way we are made to interact a reflection of the nature of God himself.

The answer is love. It is this that binds the Trinity, but also distinguishes. Each Person, Father, Son and Holy Spirit, is united with the others by a bond of love of unimaginable depth. But because it is love at its fullest and purest, each Person remains himself, and accepts the distinctions. The Son loves the Father as son loves father, and the Father accepts that love. To be fully yourself is to affirm others, and to affirm others is the way to becoming who you truly are.

Churches together

Sounds good, and you can read it in most of the better self-help books in the psychology section of a bookshop; apart from the bit about the Trinity, that is. What has it got to do with ecumenism, the relation of the different Christian churches? The simple fact is that disunity, violence and mistrust are what religion does to human beings, or, rather, what human beings do with religion. Our scattered state, within ourselves, is reflected in how we relate to others, and the closer the agenda gets to the most valuable and most damaged part of us, which is the relation to God, the more profound and damaging that reflection can become.

The conflicts and differences, however, are also potentially enriching, enlivening and redemptive. If we approach other Christians with fear, superiority, or suspicion, we are repaid in the same coin and divisions remain, and remain painful and scandalous. If we approach other Christians confident in our own faith, confident in the love of God for us and for them as human beings, confident of little else in ourselves but our tendency to conflict and disunion, there is a possibility for healing and renewed understanding; not just of institutions but of your own self. That is to be in the image of God, respecting, acknowledging difference, distinctness, while remaining united by love. It is an image we grow towards, and we shall not see its fullness in our lifetime on earth, or, indeed, in any other lifetime. The growth is the same growth as one's own progress in faith and repentance:

Dialogue also serves as an examination of conscience ... 'If we say we have not sinned, we make God a liar, and his word is not in us'

(1 John 1:10). *Such a radical exhortation to acknowledge our condition as sinners* ought also to mark the spirit we bring to ecumenical dialogue ... All the sins of the world were gathered up in the saving sacrifice of Christ, including the sins committed against the Church's unity: the sins of Christians, those of the pastors no less than those of the lay faithful. Even after the many sins which have contributed to our historical divisions, *Christian unity is possible*, provided that we are humbly conscious of having sinned against unity and are convinced of our need for conversion.

John Paul II, *Ut Unum Sint*, 34; his emphases

Such thinking makes ecumenism not merely attractive, but an essential part of being a Catholic Christian. This has to be said, since there are Catholics who think they can live in a little fortress of safe Romanism. The world, and much of the Christian world, has departed from the pure faith, and that is a problem for the world and the separated Christians. Of course we seek to welcome the strays back into the fold, and do much in terms of preaching and publishing to try and expose their errors. But *they* must be reconciled to *us*. To such as these, who think that the fault is all on the other sides, there is a challenge in the following words of St Cyprian:

God does not accept the sacrifice of a sower of disunion, but commands that he depart from the altar, so that he may first be reconciled with his brother. For God can be appeased only by prayers that make peace. To God, the better offering is peace, brotherly concord and a people made one in the unity of the Father, Son and Holy Spirit.

On the Lord's Prayer, 23

Commenting on these words, John Paul II asks, 'how can we not implore from the Lord, with renewed enthusiasm and a deeper awareness, the grace to prepare ourselves, together, to offer this *sacrifice of unity*?' (*Ut Unum Sint*, 102; his emphasis). It is not going altogether too far to say that even the Eucharist, offered in a spirit of being in the right camp, while those outside are doomed to error unless they submit, can be a sacrifice of disunion, unacceptable to God. We need to be very careful what we do, and why, if we really believe we are dealing with the God of forgiving justice and implacable love and not simply with our own internal judgements and needs.

Equally out of place is to throw differences to the winds and say we are all the same really, worshipping the same God in different ways. Ways are only ways, they do not matter that much. Let us all be one. That would be lovely and totally false. For we are not the same, none of us is the same. This is not a tragedy, but a fact of creation, that you are not me. The same applies on the level of churches. If you are a Catholic and I am a Catholic, then our differences and similarities are such that we are both called to Christ within the Roman communion. But maybe you have been called along a different path. For example, I am a monk, and you are probably not a monk. Why are we different? Because of family, upbringing, tendency to favour certain ideas over others, different desires and needs. The same recipe can make someone else a Lutheran or a Methodist.

Where do you draw the line though? We are talking here about toleration, that much-missed virtue. In our Christian history are heap upon heap of intolerance, offence both given and taken, prejudice, complacency, indifference, Pharisaism, libertarianism, misunderstandings both justified and wilful, good starts, mistakes, aspirations, betrayals, relativism and hope.

> *What is needed is a calm, clear-sighted and truthful vision of things,* a vision enlivened by divine mercy and capable of freeing people's minds and of inspiring in everyone a renewed willingness, precisely with a view to proclaiming the Gospel to the men and women of every people and nation.
>
> John Paul II, *Ut Unum Sint*, 2; his emphasis

That is not a bad definition of toleration. It is all an issue of truth. There are the truths of faith: Incarnation, Trinity, sacraments, Marian doctrine, etc. There is also the truth which grounds them, and which they try to express, the call to all people to return in trust to their God. There is also the vocation of the Church: that Christ may walk with each person the path of life. Clinging to the truths of faith in fear of others is not living in the truth. Abandoning what one knows to be true in faith for the sake of not hurting feelings or trying to express fundamental human unity is not living in the truth. Accepting that someone else is someone else and that there is nothing I can or should do about that, except love them and try to witness to the values of the Gospel, is to live in an unsatisfactory, scandalous and probably sinful world, but it is to live in the truth. The acceptance involves respect for the difference of the other. This is neither defensive posturing nor papering over of cracks. A Lutheran is a Lutheran. To minimize the difference between her and me is to show scant respect for her or for her religious tradition.

In conclusion, we might question the aims of ecumenism. Is it really desirable that we should all live under one institutional umbrella? In the most important sense, of course it is. The Church of Christ should be one and undivided, and one day will be. But what about now, as we live in a fallen world? At what stage of the family row are we? Maybe we are no further than beginning to recognize that something has gone wrong, that we are not necessarily completely in the right and the others are simply behaving in a bizarre manner showing little integrity. It takes a long time to heal a family tree, and the process is not speeded by any attempt simply to write off the past. We all have much to forgive and be forgiven. Gradually theologians are working out agreed formulae on revelation and justification; authority and sacraments will take much longer. East and West are talking after a thousand-year stand-off. There is much to look forward to, much to start. If we can have confidence in our own tradition and respect for that of others, the process will go neither too slowly nor too fast.

> The kingdom of God is like a mustard seed which at the time of its sowing in the soil is the smallest of the seeds on earth; yet once it is sown it grows into the biggest shrub of them all and puts out big branches so that the birds of the air can shelter in its shade.
>
> Mark 4:30-1

In the next chapter we shall look at one way in which the Catholic Church seems to be trying to pour weedkiller on it.

Chapter 17

INTERCOMMUNION

They cry, 'Where is bread and wine,' as they faint like wounded men.

Lamentations 2:12

Here is a difficult text for a difficult subject. It comes from Jesus' parable about a banquet. A king invites guests to a feast to celebrate the wedding of his son. All of them find excuses at the last moment not to come, and so the servants are sent to bring in anyone they find on the streets.

And those servants went out into the streets and gathered all whom they found, both bad and good; so the wedding hall was filled with guests.

But when the king came in to look at the guests, he saw there a man who had no wedding garment; and he said to him, 'Friend, how did you get in here without a wedding garment?' And he was speech-less. Then the king said to the attendants, 'Bind him, hand and foot, and cast him into the outer darkness; there, men will weep and gnash their teeth.' For many are called, but few are chosen.

Matthew 22:1–10

It is a difficult text because it undermines our faith. This Jesus, the man who said 'Come to me, all you who labour' suddenly compares the kingdom of heaven to a man being thrown out of a party because he is not in black tie. Worse than that, the man is punished, banished to the outer darkness.

Of course, most of us are quite capable of behaving like that ourselves. Every day, we throw people out of our lives. This can be very obvious, or more subtle. A good way to while away a bus or train or tube journey is to try and catch your unconscious thoughts about the other people: walkmans, mobile phones, kids, people who can do the crossword ...

St Paul was quite aware of this tendency and provided an antidote: 'Welcome one another, as Christ has welcomed you'. He did not add, 'but only if they have wedding garments on'. Hence the problem. Our faith, and sometimes our life, is built on the unconditional love of God. Christ has welcomed you, whoever and whatever. He did not come to call the righteous, but sinners. The worse you are, the more he wants you at his banquet. As we have seen, that love is brought to us in Jesus' self-sacrifice in the Eucharist, and given to us in his Body and Blood. He wants us to bring everyone we can find, 'both bad and good', to the feast. Surely there is no 'but'.

But ... the Church has rules about almost everything. We have seen why in previous chapters, and also why some of them are actually necessary. Try this one for size.

> When, in the bishop's judgement, a grave necessity arises, Catholic ministers may give the sacraments of Eucharist, Penance, and Anointing of the Sick to other Christians not in full communion with the Catholic Church, who ask of them for their own will, provided they give evidence of holding the Catholic faith regarding those sacraments, and possess the required dispositions.
>
> *Catechism of the Catholic Church*, 1401

If you have never encountered or thought about this issue before, then read that extract again, and ponder its implications. We have talked about the sacrament of Penance as the bottomless sea into which God throws all our sins. All you have to do is let him do it; that is called contrition. But here, there are conditions for approaching the unconditional mercy of God; a price to pay for the priceless Blood of Jesus. God will forgive anything, of anyone, at any time; and the Church adds: 'When, in the bishop's judgement ...' If that seems a bit odd to you, you are dead right.

However, if it seems to you to be only common sense, and you think that of course non-Catholics cannot receive our communion, a young man here poses a question for you.

Chris, a non-Catholic, has been happily married to Yvonne for nearly ten years. They have a boy, Peter, aged six, and a girl, Lucy, aged nine. Yvonne has to work on Sunday, so Chris brings the kids to the eleven o'clock Mass. They sit at the back and are sometimes quiet and absorbed in picture books, but he makes sure they follow the main parts of the liturgy. On Mondays, he and Yvonne attend, with Peter, a group preparing for first holy communion. To Chris it is very important that the children grow up with strong faith, and next Sunday, he will watch proudly as Peter receives the Body and Blood of Christ for the first time. Chris will receive communion too, having asked the priest, who obtained the Bishop's permission.

'Well, why doesn't he become a Catholic if it means that much to him?' On the other hand, 'If it means that much to him, what more can you ask?'

The question of sacramental sharing is not a theological one, to be dealt with by joint commissions and agreed statements. Nor is it the preserve of ecumaniacs. It is, for many people, a practical source of pain at the heart of their family lives. Chris and Yvonne are delighted, now. If you think that is the happy ending, where pastoral sense and charity have triumphed at last, then listen to Anne.

Anne is the sixth child of a large and traditional Catholic family. When she was seventeen, she married Paul, and they had two children. Paul was made redundant from his manual job, and repeatedly failed to keep any other job; he was becoming an alcoholic. To try and meet the bills, Anne took some cleaning jobs, which kept her out of the house most days. She grew to dread Paul coming home at night, drunk and violent. Eventually she ran away to her mother, and obtained an uncontested divorce. A few years later, she met Bill, and they have now been happily together for ten years since their civil wedding. They have custody of Paul's kids, and one of their own. Anne knows that the Church teaches that she cannot receive communion while she is living with Bill, despite their stable relationship. Over the years she has come to accept this, and finds consolation in raising her children in the Church. Their child, Darren, is due to make his first holy communion next Sunday, along with Peter. And when she sees Chris going up with his son, to receive communion ...

Anne's case demonstrates that opposition to intercommunion is not always the product of bigotry, but of genuine and justified pain. In this case, the rules have in fact been followed, but one should add that well-meaning 'pastoral' attempts by clergy or others to bend or ignore rules for the sake of one person can do even more harm to someone else.

If that is kept in mind, then the theological issues can be looked at in a proper context. Here, we are interested in sacramental sharing between Catholics and those such as Anglicans and Methodists. A very different situation obtains with the Eastern Orthodox churches, where there is much less difference over doctrine. Catholics may freely share sacraments with these churches, though they are advised to ask them first. Note that we talk of 'sacramental sharing'. What has to be said about intercommunion, has also to be said about Anointing and Penance; it is just that communion is the 'live' issue, and the clearest.

What are the rules?

Let us see what the situation is, and then try to see why. There is a lot of confusion over the issues, and accordingly much unnecessary grief or fear. The situation in the United Kingdom has been clarified recently by the Catholic Bishops' Conferences in their teaching document *One Bread, One Body*. The following are full quotations from it, answering the three most common questions. Remember that the norms apply only to the validly baptized, and that other countries have their own local regulations.

May non-Catholics ever receive communion?
Catholic ministers may lawfully administer the sacraments only to Catholic members of Christ's faithful, who equally may lawfully receive them only from Catholic ministers.

One Bread, One Body, n. 101, quoting Canon 844

Are there no exceptions?
Communion may be given to baptized Christians of other faith communities if there is a danger of death, or if there is some other grave and pressing need. This may at times include those who ask to receive them on a unique occasion for joy or for sorrow in the life of a family or an individual. It is for the diocesan bishop or his delegate

to judge the gravity of the need and the exceptional nature of the situation. The conditions of Canon Law must always be fulfilled. The exceptional nature and purpose of the permission should be made clear, and appropriate preparation should be made for the reception of the sacrament.

One Bread, One Body, n. 106

The conditions of Canon Law are the same as those quoted from the *Catechism* above. The Christian must ask of his or her own will, with evidence of holding the Catholic faith regarding the sacrament, and possess the required dispositions.

The bishops go on to identify some of the possible occasions:

- parent of a child to be baptized or receive First Communion
- parent or wife of someone being ordained
- close family at a Funeral Mass
- those confined to institutions, such as hospitals, with no access to their own ministers.

They stress, however, that these are only examples of possible cases. There is no general permission to give out communion. In addition, it should be stressed that the initiative lies with the Christian in question, and that the bishop gives the consent. There is no warrant for priests to offer invitations, or to decide cases, except when there is danger of death. The reason for this will be explored in a moment.

May Catholics ever receive communion in another Church?
Whenever necessity requires or a general spiritual advantage commends it, and provided the danger of error and indifferentism is avoided, Christ's faithful for whom it is physically or morally impossible to approach a Catholic minister may lawfully receive Holy Communion, and the sacraments of Reconciliation and Anointing of the Sick, from ministers in other faith communities whose sacraments are accepted as valid by the Catholic Church.

One Bread, One Body, n. 116, cf. Canon 844

Before you rush out, the sting is in the tail. It excludes all the Christian communities which have their origins or inspiration in the Protestant Reformation. If you are Catholic, you should not receive communion at an Anglican eucharist.

Why bother about validity?

That may well seem to be going too far. One can, perhaps, take it on board that people not in full communion with the Catholic Church should not be offered sacraments without condition. But to refuse to go to communion somewhere else seems gratuitously insulting, and a real setback to grassroots unity. The Catholic may have no confusion in his mind that the other church does not believe in the Real Presence and the transformation of the bread and wine in the same way that Catholics do. To go up and receive seems a good way of crossing an institutional division. For, say, Methodists, the communion symbolizes God's love for us, and ours for each other. Why cannot a Catholic receive communion on those terms?

An answer may lie in an understanding of what we mean by 'validity'. It is more than the rather childish concept that 'they aren't allowed to do that'. Validity of sacrament involves two much deeper ideas.

- Sacraments do not belong to us. They are given, each time, to believers by Jesus himself, acting through his ministers. We don't make the Eucharist, we receive the communion. While God can act in any way through anyone, the sacraments are a special space which he has promised us, given through specially chosen ministers, ordained (which means changed, as well as appointed). Other churches do not believe, by and large, in sacraments at this level.
- Sacraments are not just for me. This is the idea of communion: an unconditional surrender of ourselves to God in and with each other. The Eucharist links us to all Catholics throughout space and time. By our confirmation and communion, we are changed into being part of that body. It is not an institutional organization or society, but a living body. As such, when we communicate, we do so not as ourselves, but as the whole Body of Christ. When another church is not in full communion, we cannot, individually, become united simply by sharing an action.

I don't really expect that will persuade anyone. But it is important to realize that the bishops' position is not simple cruelty or unintelligent bigotry. It comes from the basic principles of our faith, and we have to listen to them, even if we cannot agree. If in doubt, see chapter 12 on 'How to Disagree with the Pope'.

How can we say no?

'Surely Jesus would not have bothered about all this. He preached a message of love and tolerance, not institution and rivalry. He would not refuse anyone communion.'

This is true, to the extent that the Eucharist does not belong to the Church to offer or withhold at will. Even less does it belong to any individual priest to refuse the sacraments to someone or to say that the rules do not matter at all in this special case. There is a question of truth involved, however. Either the bread and wine become the Body and Blood of Christ in the sense taught by Catholics, or they do not. Either one believes this, or not. To say 'Amen' and receive communion is to assent to that truth and so receive its benefits. Taking the Eucharist as any less than it is, even for the best of reasons, is not quite what it is about. So, the Church does lay down conditions for reception, so that people can decide whether, in conscience, they ought to ask a blessing, instead of communicating. The assumption is surely warranted that someone holding out their hands to Christ genuinely wants him and loves him, and believes that he is there. Confusion arises from poor catechesis, which is not the fault of the person seeking communion.

We have to deal with the fact that Jesus threw someone out of the banquet for not wearing the right clothes. Much as one might wish he had not, he did. Nor did he seem to be much into symbolic gestures, or a false love that says all is well even as the ship is sinking.

At this point, we have to confront the pain of the issue.

> We are called to be one, and we seek more urgently than ever before to be one band of pilgrims, united in faith and love, in holiness and in mission. This makes us feel even more strongly the pain of our divisions, above all at the Eucharist where we are unable to share together as one Body the one Bread of Life.
>
> *One Bread, One Body*, n. 76

The Bishops then point out that this pain can be a powerful driving force for real unity. The simple desire to remove a sense of sorrow and hurt is not enough for full unity. Between the separated

4

churches there are many years of deep wounds and wounding; it would be wrong to pretend they are not there. When they are healed, we can come together in eucharistic communion, and our joy will be complete.

One could push this point further, and say that not receiving each other's communion is a genuine expression and reflection of our incomplete unity. It is an expression of full respect for the other's differences. As such, it is almost sacramental in itself; non-communion *is* our state of communion. After all, trying to hide our differences is not unlike an individual hiding his or her sins from God. In both cases, he cannot heal the wounds unless we open them to him in the cold air of truth. If unity is to be the work of God, and not a patch-up just for our time, then we have to offer him ourselves as we really are. The state of affairs envisioned by the bishops is a sign of where we are now, and the pain is a sign of where we are going together. On this way, there are many things we can do, and these must not be neglected in pursuit of something for which we are not, as churches, ready. And, of course, to say or imply that I or my little group of Christians is ahead of our various denominations on this and so can do what we wish is to stretch very thin my own bonds of communion with my own church which I am leaving 'behind'.

As a final word, I must re-emphasize that although the issue of intercommunion is a matter of theology and negotiation and relationships between institutions and communities, the real impact is in real families: your family and my family. There is as little excuse for insensitive prohibition as there is for facile pastorality. The pain and difficulties must be shared and worked through, and the right solutions and tolerations found for each and all. Even if we cannot be fully one in faith and sacrament, we must not allow ourselves or others to faint out of hunger for Christian love.

PART 4

ISSUES FOR TODAY

Chapter 18

THE BETTER PART

In the image of God, male and female, he created them.

Genesis 1:27

Christians are people who look backwards in history, but that does not mean that they are backward themselves. We look to the past because the past contains events which, we believe, changed for all time the relation between human beings and God, and between human beings and each other. We look to the past because the events of our Christian past can play a part in our struggle to find meaning in the present.

Religion is not about avoiding problems; at the heart of our faith is a crucifixion, a wasteful and cruel human death. Christianity is about how we face and try to resolve the inevitable problems and woes of life. It is about finding and showing to others the presence of Christ in all that seems to hide or deny him, in all that seeks to extinguish our love for each other and for God. In this section we will look at some contemporary problem areas. It is not my intention to propose any solutions or to push a particular viewpoint. I simply want to demonstrate a way of approach that seeks to preserve the bonds of charity while not minimizing pain and difficulty. The subjects ahead include suicide and the despair of loneliness, the threat or promise of scientific research, the sense of meaninglessness or rejection that can be felt by unemployed, disabled or elderly people or indeed anybody else, how we might react to the sharp fall in numbers of priests, and the urgent need to find for women a valued and dignified place within the Church.

It is with much hesitation that I write about this last topic. The last hundred years or so have seen many fundamental changes in human life, from weapons of mass destruction to organ transplants, but the most significant and far reaching will perhaps have been the discovery by one half of the species that the other half is human too. This discovery was not made without some hesitation and reluctance. Men, by and large, had to be persuaded that women are their equals, and their attention had to be caught by protest and demonstration. Nor is the process over. Women are still under-represented in most professions and company hierarchies. Men still write letters to the London *Times* beginning with 'My wife thinks ...'

What about the Church? Some would say that the process has not even begun. Women are, by definitive papal statement, barred from being priests, or even deacons. The structures of Church government remain male, in personnel, outlook and assumption. The liturgy and many Church documents remain, except perhaps in the USA, phrased in what is now seen as exclusive language. Small concessions (in England and Wales we say that Christ's blood 'will be shed for you and for all' instead of the previous 'for all men') simply highlight the bigger problem. Yet, if you look round a church on Sundays, hold a census of people who do things around the parish, and count those who go on retreats, women outnumber men, sometimes by quite a lot.

Whether you think the Church is far behind the times or keeping up quite well is a matter of opinion, and differences of opinion have always been a legitimate part of Catholic life. However, facts are also quite interesting, and so is the drift of more recent papal and other official statements about women in the Church. It is worth avoiding, so far as possible, extremes of language and assumption. To be militantly feminist and not listen to anything else is not much more helpful than being obsessively chauvinist and not listening to what women have to say. This is not the place to enter into debate about how far, if anywhere, political correctness can take us, or what parts of the Church's vocabulary are impossibly tainted with the memory of oppressive androcentrism, the domination of men and male language and perspectives.

Let us agree, though, that no single group in the Church, however large, has the right or authority of itself to alienate or leave behind other groups. This is quite a live issue in parishes where some find the exclusive language of authorized Bible translations to be offensive. It is a simple matter for a reader to substitute 'people' for 'men' or 'him and her' for 'him' and so on. But what if that irritates lots of other people? By trying to get things right you have divided a parish. It is not a straightforward and obvious question which should prevail.

What is obvious is that all sides should hear each other and bear with each other in charity, be prepared to give way and forgive. If not, then your zeal is not godly, and your cause is not Christ's, however right it may seem, or indeed may be. If that sounds too harsh, the same goes for groups within parishes that sometimes like to take over, and impose on others a particular spirituality or view of things. I will not name any names for fear of being unfair, but if it has happened in your parish you will know what I mean.

There is rarely any harm in listening, though. This means that there is also little harm in talking, provided we speak the truth in love. Some people have the idea that it is wrong to 'speak out' in the Church, to campaign or press for any change, that everything should be left to authority to decide as seems wise. But if that is indeed the case, it is also wrong to speak out in favour of the status quo. We do all, in fact, have a duty not only to listen to the magisterium (the teaching Church) but also to speak to it. In terms of historical fact, the Church has almost always moved in response to the needs and rights of the faithful.

This has almost always been painfully slow, barring the occasional inspired revolutions such as Vatican II, Lateran IV or Pentecost. The slowness comes from the fact that the Church is Catholic; all must be accommodated across the whole world, even if that may mean heroic patience on the part of those who consider themselves 'ahead'. It is sometimes even a personal sacrifice to put up with it, but that is a price to be paid for being in a tolerant community which, as well as the stick-in-the-muds, tolerates you. Nor is it simply sticking in the mud, institutional inertia, that makes things slow. Sometimes what is good for a part is not good for all, and so cannot become universal practice; which often means it cannot be practice anywhere. To take an example, theological issues apart, the ordination of women would not necessarily have the positive impact in some societies that it would in the emancipated West.

But that does not mean that we are meant to bury what we know to be unjust or think to be wrong. We have to keep speaking, and the accumulated force of all our voices, if we speak in the right way, will be the breath of the Holy Spirit directing the barque of Peter towards the right shore. That is how it has always worked, within our very considerable sinful limitations, and how it will always work if we do not lose courage.

If listening and talking are the way forward, it is not for me to try to speak for Catholic women. In this chapter I will simply put forward some of the recent Church thinking on women's issues for you to consider and react to. First we will look at general principles and then, in the next chapter, consider the issue of women and priesthood.

Not women but people

The subtitle is intended as a caution against speaking too generally about any group of people. The tendency can be to forget, without realizing it, that one is talking about people, not objects or categories. The first thing to be said is that each human person, male or female, must be taken as him or herself, as a unique expression of the creative love of God. Nothing must obscure that, even in the cause of justice. Each person has a right to authentic human development, without hindrance. This principle underlies most Catholic teaching on ethics, and can also be found at the heart of the UN Declaration on Human Rights.

It seems indisputable, but is not as benign as it appears. For if each human person has a right to authentic growth, they have a right to development of who they are, of themselves. That means *themselves*, not as part of a grouping, cultural or political or otherwise. You have a fundamental God-given right to be you, and I have a right to be me. No power on earth can legitimately constrain me to become like you or you like me, and no divine power is going to either. If I am Afro-Caribbean, and you are Eurasian, then that is part of who each of us is, and neither of us can negate what is part of the other, be it by discrimination or any other means. The same is true of the sexes; women have a right to grow into authentic womanhood, and men into a truly masculine expression of human nature before God. Hence, the Second Vatican Council noted with enthusiastic approval that

The hour is coming, in fact has come, when the vocation of woman is being achieved in its fullness, the hour in which woman acquires in the world an influence, an effect and a power never hitherto achieved.

Message to Women, 13–14

The moral evil of discrimination must not be confused with legitimate difference. Argument can and does turn on what is and is not legitimate difference; the mistakes are easy to make and hard to undo. In the United Kingdom, it was self-evident to most men in the nineteenth century that women should not be able to vote in elections and that India should be ruled by the British. History has shown both these positions to be oppressive rather than part of the natural state of things. In these cases, discrimination had been disguised as difference. But you can do it the other way with equally disastrous results; take as an example the misery in developing countries caused by expecting them to function as advanced economies and cope with loans and buying expensive weapons.

In its slow way, the Church is concerned that the pursuit of proper equality between the sexes should not destroy some very precious facts about the differences between them. This is even becoming reflected in general culture as books are produced trying to help men recover their own identity in the face of demoralization following the entirely right and just promotion of women into full citizen and employment rights. In particular, there are many things special to women that are closed to men. The trouble is that all these things have been misused to try and stem the advance of feminism, including childbearing, sensitivity of temperament, particular mental and survival skills and being beautiful. But a truth misused does not cease to be true. The Church has a task of rescuing such truths from their kidnappers and putting them back in context.

For example, the most stunning and important event of all time happened through a woman.

Mary is the only human person who eminently fulfils God's plan of love for humanity ... Every woman shares in some way in her sublime dignity.

John Paul II, *General Audience*, 29 November 1995

That can be taken the wrong way, and often is, to mean that Mary represents submission and meekness. She has an auxiliary role, to produce the male Messiah and then stand back and let him do the real work. Her place is in the home at Nazareth, the pious embodiment of a confined domestic role that no woman with spirit would put up with today. This is often what is said, but it is not what the Church means at its best. John Paul II continues:

> Mary, on the contrary, is the model of the full development of woman's vocation, since, despite the objective limits imposed by her social condition, she exercised a vast influence on the destiny of humanity and the transformation of society.

In other words, a woman having been at the centre of the central event of history, an event that would not and could not have happened without her active consent and participation, nobody has a leg to stand on in saying that women lack any value, any dignity, and no society should exist which does not do justice to that value.

For the Church to say so would not only be to contradict the facts of salvation history, but also the facts of life, and to express the deepest ingratitude to the women who have played and do play in many cases the vital part in our life, both as individuals, male and female, and as a church. If one must talk of value and importance, it is not clear that men prevail over women. One could mention the great feminine saints, who include military leaders, judges, abbesses, academics, politicians such as Isabel of Portugal, Hilda of Whitby, or Catherine of Siena. But that is just to mention the contributions that even men could make, even if it demonstrates that in the long years of discrimination the Church was one of the few places for a woman to get on in life. Far less obvious, but also far more valuable, is the silent witness of women who have simply lived and given of what they have to the human race: mothers, sisters, daughters, human beings expressing God's love.

It raises the question of who leads the Church, and who has led it; which people in fact have and hold power in Christ's community. In a hierarchical sense it is the clergy, who control the instruments of government and are charged with dispensing the sacraments. But there is more than politics and administration to life. Speaking to a group of young Parisians, John Paul II had this to say, and I leave it for your own consideration. I am reluctant to say more, since it is for a woman to respond to what is said to women.

> Just as it is true that the Church, in the hierarchical sense, is direct-
> ed by the successors of the Apostles, and therefore by men, it is cer-
> tainly all the more true that, in the charismatic sense, women 'lead'
> her as much, and perhaps even more.
>
> *Address*, 1 June 1980

But is there really any reason why a priesthood could not be both authentically masculine and feminine? What is said so far does not imply that women should not be successors of the apostles. Such a question belongs in the next chapter, in a discussion of priesthood and ministry in the Church today.

Chapter 19

WORTH A MASS?

Should he open, no one shall close.

Isaiah 22:22

In 1968, in the United States, there were 35,925 priests, 8,325 graduate-level seminarians in training for ordination and just under 180,000 religious sisters working in various orders across the country. According to the United States Catholic Conference, the respective figures in 1998 were 31,657, 3,158, and 85,412. The average age of priests in 1996 was fifty-eight, and of nuns and sisters sixty-nine. In the same thirty-year period, the number of parishes without a resident priest almost quintupled to 2,460. By contrast, the number of Catholics in the US grew roughly in line with general growth of population, from 46.6 to 61.6 million, which is just under a quarter of all Americans.

If the figures speak for themselves, we have a crisis. The pattern is replicated in most of the 'developed' countries, though not always as severely. And there are occasional pockets of good news, most notably in some contemplative houses of monks and nuns. What is going on? It is unlikely that any one factor is responsible for such a large change. Certainly, many priests left the priesthood and religious brothers and sisters their orders in the difficult years after the Second Vatican Council. It is also true that some institutions and dioceses made mistakes in recruitment, formation and general policy which might have precipitated their own decline. But with such a general and marked trend, it is simplistic to say that the Second Vatican Council, and the changes it brought, were to blame for the decline in vocations, in the numbers of people feeling a call to priesthood or religious life. Society has changed too in the last fifty years; in many ways it has changed more radically than the Church.

Perhaps the most obvious change, though one often missed, is that it is now possible to do as a job, and as a reasonably well paid or respected job, tasks that used to be done by priests or religious, especially sisters. These include nursing and teaching, but also the 'social work' aspects of parish work. Opportunities for voluntary work overseas have multiplied, and there are now many umbrella groups which cater for this; for example, the Palms organization in Australia. Young men and women who aspire to service can find their vocation in ways other than the institutional structures of Church life, and without the obvious sacrifices of celibacy and relative poverty.

One should also say that there are now rather fewer young people than previously, coming from smaller families. This has a significant impact on vocations. A priest friend of mine once began a homily on Vocations Sunday in England by saying 'Today is the day when, all over the world, men and women devoutly pray that someone else's son will become a priest.' This is not to say that Catholic parents actively discourage vocations; it is simply that in a family with ten children more options appear than in a family with two.

There is an abiding need to get on in life. We have to be successful, as individuals and as families. Children are driven on from the age of three, or even earlier, to attain results, to acquire skills and competitive dispositions. That is how life is, and Catholic families cannot opt out of the real world. But in such a context, where the issue is getting them into a good college or university, the suggestion of leaving it all to follow Christ is unlikely even to cross one's mind. Nor are families what they were, a close group in which people learn community values and that interdependence can make us strong. Everyone is more on their own in a cold world, and they simply have to get that qualification and that job. To be successful is to make money, preferably more than your parents. One should also be free, not chained by undue commitment to other people, companies, jobs, places or lifestyle. In such a context the lifelong leap into ordained ministry or consecrated life is deeply unattractive to many. It is, once again, not their fault; it is how the world has become.

A tempting way of response is to take a leaf from the secular world's book. For the sake of simplicity, we will concentrate here on the ordained ministry of bishops, priests and deacons. If a company is having difficulties recruiting, they do a number of things, some of which have been taken on board by national Church bodies and some Orders. One advertises, communicates more effectively the nature of the business and the opportunities it offers. One tries to make the organization look exciting and appealing, by highlighting challenges and opportunities. But you could also change the job conditions: increase the salary, add benefits such as cars or medical insurance, provide more flexible working hours and so on. It is not hard to see ways in which we could do the same with vocations.

For example, there is the recruitment base. We are shortly going to lack priests in a big way, yet we accept candidates from only half the human race. Why not women? Maybe having to promise celibacy is a major turn-off. Why not let priests marry? People want some social position and an income that guarantees security. Why not allow priests to hold down normal jobs and do the sacramental side part time as needed, instead of, say, playing golf?

To some, the answers are obvious, in either the 'yes' or horrified 'no' direction. It is really too early to say what might happen, what might be done. But some options are bigger than others. A minor change such as part-time ministers would not cause too much theological angst, though it might not be so straightforward to organize. It is done with a fair amount of success in other Christian churches. To ordain women would be a far bigger step, though some would say a more urgent one. This issue involves far more than numbers, and far deeper issues, so we will treat it separately, as it deserves.

For now, we must note that the pastoral ministry of the Church has been organized in all kinds of ways in different times and places. In the modern West, where Christianity is no longer the base culture, the future may not lie in parishes, with their immediate and concentrated demands on dedicated manpower and infrastructure, but in the looser organization of mission territory. On the other hand, the lack of ordained ministers is already leading to a renewed appreciation of what ordinary parishioners can do to bring Christ to each other. Perhaps the future can be seen hopefully, with lay people realizing their full vocations within parishes and clergy being concentrated on what is specifically sacramental. Who knows? It would, however, be useful to know what can be changed and what cannot, so we shall spend a brief time looking at what priests, and bishops and deacons, actually are.

What is a priest?

One of the lesser-known facts of Christian life is that we are all priests, that we all have vocations. This is so by virtue of baptism. In this sacrament we become involved in the mission of Christ to the world, a mission to bring forgiveness of sins and to preach this good news. Baptism, as well as washing away sins, is also an incorporation into the Church. This is the most wonderful part of the humility of God incarnate. He has appointed each of us to be his Body, his presence in the world; our hands to be his, held out in friendship and forgiveness and feeding. No power of darkness can quench such a witness. But if you and I do not do it, it will not happen. This is our dignity and our duty as Christians, that God the Creator of all has left the most important tasks up to us.

You might be equal to that, but I am not. Yet there is so much to be done, so many lonely to love, so many sick to give solace to, so many poor to enrich, so many despairing to encourage, so many places crying out for peace, so many mourners longing for joy, so many confused and lost to whom we must bring faith. This is, for those who can sense another's need and their own Christ-like power to save, both a challenge and a reason to live.

> Look around you, look at the fields, already they are white, ready for the harvest. Already the reaper is being paid his wages, already he is bringing in the grain for eternal life, and thus the sower and reaper rejoice together ... The harvest is rich but the labourers are few, so ask the Lord of the harvest to send labourers to his harvest.
>
> John 4:35–7; Matthew 9:37

How can we do it, though? On our own, of course we cannot. This is not because we are not strong enough; there are all kinds of things we *can* do. It is because the ills of the human race need a different kind of strength: not force, but invitation; not demand, but sacrifice. The only source of that is the Lamb of God who gave himself to take away the sins of the world. Our mission is his mission, not ours; his message, not ours; and it is done by the power of *his* Holy Spirit.

God's saving power is found in all kinds of ways, in many places and in the most surprising people. But Christ left a way in which he promises we will find and receive it, which is the sacramental life of the Church. This life does not exclude other ways; it underpins and blesses them. The priesthood of us all, our share in the one priesthood of Christ, is enabled, reinforced and fed by the sacraments. These do not happen of themselves. They need to be given to us, brought to us. This is the reason for a *ministerial* priesthood, which has become, for better or worse, the ordained hierarchy of bishops, priests and deacons. It is vital to get this the right way round, and Catholics have not always succeeded in doing so. However:

> The ministerial priesthood is at the service of the common priesthood. It is directed at the unfolding of the baptismal grace of all Christians. The ministerial priesthood is a *means* by which Christ unceasingly builds up and leads his Church.
>
> *Catechism of the Catholic Church*, 1547

As a reminder of this, the Pope has the title 'servant of the servants of God'. Even if that title has not always been given its obvious interpretation through history, it encapsulates a key fact about priesthood. Priests are not, of themselves, the front-line troops, the 'real' Church, the pinnacle of Christ's Body, the rulers of his people. They are ancillary workers, the baggage handlers, cooks and engineers, not the army. This is not to do down the importance of priesthood – without them, the army would not move or eat. Servants, by being what they are, become indispensable, as the one priest, Jesus, pointed out: 'for who is greater, the one at table, or the one who serves? The one at table, surely? Yet here am I among you as one who serves' (Luke 22:27).

Why, though, do sacraments need ministers? Why is there a specified caste of ordained people, and why can only these dispense sacraments? It would surely be a better arrangement if any Christian could hear confessions and give absolution, could give the sacrament of anointing to the sick, or could preside at a family celebration of the Eucharist. It is not, however, that sacraments need ministers; it is that we need them.

Imagine the following rather strange world. It is just like the earth, except that for some unknown reason buried in history, human beings cannot drink the water. There is something wrong with the world's oceans and rivers and atmosphere to make this so. Often, and most of the time in some parts, it is entirely safe to drink water from springs and rivers. But it happens enough times that someone dies a painful death or is horribly ill for a few days after drinking natural water that very few trust the supply. Fortunately, someone long ago discovered a way of making water safe. It is an expensive and difficult way, requiring specialized knowledge and rather large machinery, so it is not really practicable for each home to have a plant. There are several in each town, about one plant to each three thousand of population. So, daily, people queue with pitchers, jugs and cans of water to take them to the plant to be purified and made safe and life-giving.

Those people have something we lack, which is a sense of the value of water. If you call water 'grace', you get close to the idea. We can find grace in all sorts of ways, but not always. We can do all kinds of good of ourselves, but not reliably. Our human loves and powers are not always to the good. We need help and direction. Hence each sacrament contains a liturgy of the Word, where we can listen to and learn about God's plan for salvation. That Word has special ministers – lay readers, deacons – so that we know that it is something special, not to be taken lightly or for granted. We are given grace by God through ministers so that we cannot grab it for ourselves. Nor can we grab it for others. What we take away from the sacraments – and if you are excluded from communion, what we take away simply by proximity to Christ in his sacraments – is pure love of God for humanity, untainted by any of our mixed motives. It is the real, unpolluted water of life we can pass on to others. And once again, it is to the glory of God that he often chooses the most pathetic specimens of humanity to fulfil this most vital of functions.

Why not women?

If, however, we are talking simply about function, we do not get the full picture. If priesthood is simply a job, albeit an awe-inspiring and indispensable job, then it is manifestly unfair in modern Western culture to exclude women from priesthood. It is more than unfair, it is actually morally wrong to do so.

But there is more. To be a priest is not to have a task, though there are priestly tasks. It is a way of being, a distinct way of being human. The nature of the sacraments is such that their ministers should be a consecrated order. For sacraments are not simply symbolic actions or reminders, they are the power of Christ made fully present at that time and place. The priest, in sacramental terms, does not just hand out grace, nor does he just 'stand for' Jesus. In sacramental terms, he *is* Christ, forgiving and healing. Any priest for whom that is a source of pride rather than the profoundest humility and awe needs a refresher course. Priests can, and do, get things wrong. Their lives can often witness to values that are other than those of the Gospel. They need all the help they can get, by prayer and by encouragement.

Traditionally, it is not possible for a woman to be a representative of Christ at this level, because Christ was a man. If that seems daft, and I have to say that I do not find it very persuasive, then be aware that there are people to whom it makes perfect sense. There is something in this, if not much. It is essential to Christian belief that Jesus was not an abstract 'nature' or generalized human being, but an actual person, particular, like you and me. To be a human person, you have to be either male or female. So, in some senses, it is important that Jesus was a man. But what senses these are can be a matter for argument. It would be very odd to suggest that if Jesus had dark hair, then only dark-haired men could be priests, since only they represented fully the particularity of the Incarnation. On the other hand, you might say that masculinity and femininity are more fundamental to being a person than hair colour, and so one should pay this argument more respect.

But tradition is not something to be lightly set aside, even if it can always be questioned in the light of Christian experience. The current Church position is for no change. John Paul II has gone so far as to say that he cannot see how the Church has authority to set aside Christ's historical choice of men only to be consecrated as apostles. In his letter *Ordinatio Sacerdotalis* of May 1994, a letter which intended to close discussion of the subject, the Pope added:

> Furthermore, the fact that the Blessed Virgin Mary, Mother of God and Mother of the Church, received neither the mission proper to the Apostles nor the ministerial priesthood clearly shows that the non-admission of women to priestly ordination cannot mean that women are of a lesser dignity, nor can it be construed as discrimination against them.

Ordinatio Sacerdotalis, 3

You can say that this choice was itself culturally conditioned, and that the early history of the Church is not so clear at all, and that would be perfectly reasonable and possibly true. But the Church, as stated before, is a slow mover, even if it is generally sure.

There are a number of reasons why movement should be slow in this case, though. The movement for the ordination of women is based on a call for equality. It takes priesthood as something that either men or women could do, and that women are therefore unjustly debarred from. After all, in the culture of the first century, it made sense for the Word to become flesh as a man, and for him to have appointed male apostles, though one should note that women played a key role in Jesus' life and ministry too. Today, the situation is very different, and there is no longer such a cultural impediment to women taking a full and equal role to men. To say that the sexes are complementary, not identical, that the equal body of humanity is divided into two different parts, equal in value though not in function, temperament or sensitivity, is only half an answer to this. We cannot say what a woman would bring to priesthood; maybe a priesthood containing both genders would be richer than a single-sex hierarchy, precisely because men and women are so different.

It would be a desperate shame if a successful campaign for women's ordination destroyed one of the key planks of the Council's renewal. This was the separation of orders and power, the realization that priesthood is not about rank or privilege; or that if it is, it is about service and coming last. To interpret the denial of orders to women as discrimination could be (I do not say 'is', because that depends on you) to see the hierarchical priesthood as a social position of privilege. While nobody with eyes in his or her head would say that the Church has got very far towards making real such a separation between ministry and social power, we can perhaps agree that it is a road worth travelling. Who knows what we will find along that road if we dare to take it. Once that separation is acknowledged then the running of the Church, the question of why only ordained men can hold certain kinds of power – a position still enshrined in canon law – becomes more open. If a feminist solution ends up reinforcing outdated images of domination, then it is worse than the problem.

Ordination is not a right for anyone. If a man wants to be a priest, there is a careful process of assessment and selection, followed by a long period of training and formation. The point of all that is to discover if he is really called, by God, to the priesthood; such a call emerges strongly in the inevitable ups and downs of seminary or religious life. If there is a vocation, everything else works out; there are, for example, many fine priests who did not shine in their studies, but whose other qualities marked them out as men of prayer and pastoral gift. Anyone who feels women should be ordained, therefore, has to ask themselves a searching question. Is it a matter of rights, or of vocation; of politics, or of grace? It is quite possible, even very likely, that women today do feel genuinely called to priesthood. The Church should listen to them. But the gift of orders is a gift within the community; a harsh reality that affects men as well, though not to the same extent.

I am not saying any of this is decisive argument. It is simply important to be clear about what one wants and why. We are not dealing with human, but divine realities, and there is much to get wrong. The Church is often faced with choosing the path of least harm rather than what is right; such is our world. But in case you feel that the ordination of women would be a final disaster in the Kingdom of God, there is a point worth bearing in mind, and it is well made by John Paul II in his 1995 *Letter to Priests*:

> The Second Vatican Council grasped the logic of the Gospel ... when it presented the Church first as the People of God and only after-wards as a hierarchical structure. The Church is first and foremost the People of God, since all her members, men and women alike, share each in his or her specific way in the prophetic, priestly and royal mission of Christ.

There already are women priests. What we do not have are women ministerial priests. More than that, the hierarchy is not an essential part of the Church; it is not what the Church is. The structure is simply how it has happened; it has advantages and disadvantages. If the Holy Spirit guides us, slowly, at the only pace we seem to be able to cope with, towards a different structure, even radically different, then the Church itself remains as it was; it is just expressed differently. No organizational fact about the Church is set in tablets of stone, except that we are the People of God. We need have no fear of a changed future if that is the will of God. If we do fear, it is not fear of God; our opposition is not theological.

So, opponents of women's ordination need to be as careful as supporters, perhaps more so. With that in mind, it should be hoped that no pressure for ordination of women will be allowed to detract from the wider agenda of finding ways in which both men and women can live and flourish in the Church, giving to each other and to all of their gifts. That is our task. And we should note that women have an advantage, a number of special gifts in the Christian community that we are only starting to recognize.

God knows where they will lead. This is a source of courage, not of holding back. The same papal text notes, for example, 'Beneath the cross there is only one Apostle, John, the son of Zebedee, whereas there are several women ... And it is they who will be the first to go to the tomb ... they will be the ones to tell the Apostles.' If we do not listen to Catholic women, we may miss an equally important message.

Chapter 20

LIVING IN SIN

Does one plough the sea with oxen?

Amos 6:11

This chapter is not simply about sexuality. It is about human relationships, and what makes them healthy and fulfilling. More than any other, the issue of marriage and sexual ethics brings the Church into disrepute, and makes Catholics look ridiculous. It has caused more real torment than almost any other set of questions. Almost every papal encyclical, every book published on the faith is assessed by reviewers on what it has to say about contraception. (Indeed, have you joined our conversation midstream by turning to this chapter first?) In the media mind, Catholicism is identified with a set of bizarre, outdated sexual taboos.

The same is true for many a Catholic mind as well. Perhaps we ignore what we know the Church teaches about artificial birth control. This can result in all kinds of inner conflict. It is not easy lightly to set aside the opinion of the magisterium, and then be free of all confusion and guilt. Nor, once you start, is it always easy to stop, and people drift away, scandalized by the Church of Christ. The hot issue here has always been contraception, but another area has come to the fore more recently, which we will consider as an example of an approach.

For example

The Church does not always help; or rather, it can seem to be at fault here. It is not just a matter of being out of date or repressive.

The Church can say things that make people feel their very selves are unacceptable to God. The clearest examples of this are some statements about homosexuals. But these statements can also illustrate what the Church actually teaches, as opposed to what we tend to think it does (clergy too). So we will use this issue as an example to set out the general principles.

The homosexual population is a vulnerable group at the best of times, facing the simple fear and revulsion that many people show towards them. Homosexuality has always been present in human societies, and it has almost always been disapproved of, and sometimes persecuted. Vulnerability can go in two directions. It is quite common for young men and women to end up feeling less than human, intrinsically bad, because of their sexual feelings. When these are directed primarily to the same sex, the feeling can become more acute, to the point of actual illness and even suicide. More often, the person can never quite shake off a feeling of being 'wrong'. It does not help, of course, when society shuns them with fear or loathing. This leads to the second manifestation of vulnerability, which is aggression: the gay pride movements, hostile promotion of homosexual culture, the 'outing' of key public figures and so on. If this does not really help the cause, it is at least understandable.

It also makes some sense within the Church when we are faced with statements like this:

> Basing itself on Sacred Scripture, which presents homosexual acts as acts of grave depravity, Tradition has always declared that homosexual acts are intrinsically disordered. They are contrary to the natural law. They close the sexual act to the gift of life. They do not proceed from a genuine affective and sexual complementarity. Under no circumstances can they be approved.
>
> *Catechism of the Catholic Church*, 2357

If you are convinced that this is true, then try to put yourself in the shoes of someone who knows no sexual attraction except to other men or other women. How would they react to this? How do you think they feel when they hear that the acts they desire are gravely wrong, against the whole order of things? What then do they conclude about themselves?

And what does the Church offer them? A rare and lofty vocation, which, if fulfilled, can lead to the heights of sanctity:

> Homosexual persons are called to chastity. By the virtues of self-
> mastery that teach them inner freedom, at times by the support of
> disinterested friendship, by prayer and sacramental grace, they can,
> and should, gradually and resolutely approach Christian perfection.
>
> *Catechism of the Catholic Church*, 2359

All are called to chastity, without exception. Chastity is simply the virtue of loving another for their own sake. Few heterosexuals are called to celibacy, an exclusive bond of love with Christ. But the Church seems to say that for all homosexuals the only form of chastity is in complete abstinence. This raises the stakes in terms of what is meant by moral failure. Only the fullest holiness of life can expunge their intrinsic disorder.

Such a way of thinking is unfortunate, because it closes rather than opens the doors of the Church. It leads to a prohibition of active homosexuals from receiving communion and being absolved from sin unless they show a determination to fight their disorder. Yet how many 'straight' sexual relationships, even within a long and successful marriage, live up to the ideal and are free of exploitation and simple lust? Surely, there is no solid line to be drawn; if you have to be that good to be part of the sacramental life of the Church, it might seem that none of us should go up for communion.

Chapter 15 looks at how you might survive if you are barred from communion. Here, we need to see how the Church has begun to respond to charges of injustice and homophobia. It has to be said that these charges have some justification, even if they can be carried too far in violence. But we need to look beyond the outrage to the actual content of the Catholic faith. There is much that is positive even in documents that fall far short of what some would wish:

> It is deplorable that homosexual persons have been and are the subject of violence in speech or in action. Such treatment deserves condemnation from the Church's pastors wherever it occurs. It reveals a kind of disregard for others which endangers the most fundamental principles of a healthy society. The intrinsic dignity of each person must always be respected in word, in action and in law.
>
> Congregation for the Doctrine of the Faith, *Pastoral Care of Homosexual Persons*, 10

People not sorts

I have presented the offence and anguish that the wording of the Catechism and other Church documents can cause. The Church seems to be put on the same side as all the homophobes and queer-bashers of history. Certainly, the Church does not lack such people; as a fallen society one expects it to contain slightly above the general population average of bigots, fools and hypocrites. But the faith is richer than that, and some of that richness is expressed in recent publications by the magisterium, including the Congregation for the Doctrine of the Faith's *Letter on the Pastoral Care of Homosexual Persons*. I go into detail on this issue because it illustrates a principle that can be applied to many others, including contraception and cohabitation.

One thing to say straight away is that the Church generally opposes strict labelling, since this can imprison rather than define. Sexuality, in particular, is an odd, poorly understood phenomenon. Orientation is rarely absolutely one way or the other, and can indeed change through life and in different circumstances. For example, it is quite normal for adolescents and young adults to have homosexual and heterosexual feelings for different people; what used to be called 'having a crush'. This is true for both boys and girls, and a cause of much unnecessary angst. To insist that someone decides from earliest puberty whether they are homo or hetero is eventually to deny them full human freedom. To see only the label, and to talk only in the language and agenda of labels, is to miss the point. This is important, because being human, and fully human, is the only thing God really asks of us, and the context for seeing any difficulty, be it sexual or financial:

The human person, made in the image and likeness of God, can hardly be adequately described by a reductional reference to his or her sexual orientation. Everyone living on the face of the earth has personal problems and difficulties, but has challenges to growth, strengths, talents and gifts as well. Today the Church provides a badly needed context for the care of the human person when she refuses to consider the person as *heterosexual or homosexual* and insists that each person has a fundamental identity: a creature of God, and by grace, his child and heir to eternal life.

Congregation for the Doctrine of the Faith, *Pastoral Care of Homosexual Persons*, 16; emphasis added

Surprisingly sensible, isn't it? Keep it in mind, as we have to consider the biting part. It is tough, in fact, for everyone. Catholic teaching on sex comes from two principles. The first principle is that genital expression of sexual love belongs within marriage. The second is that such expression must be open to the possibility of transmitting life, to the conception of a child. Neither of these makes much sense on its own, but both are invariably taken out of their setting and turned into simple prohibitions. The setting is a vision of what human relationships are about. Human love shows us a reflection of the very nature of God. Hence sexuality is to do with relationship, and the moral quality of sex is proportioned to the quality of relationship, the depth of love.

There are many forms of love, some better reflectors than others. My putting up with a rather boring conversation for the sake of borrowing your ladder is a fairly low reflection. The shared love of two people who have committed themselves to each other and to no others, without condition for the rest of their lives, is a much better image of the love of the Trinity. If that love is open to creation then the image is at its clearest, and we little creatures can share in the awesome power of God to create life out of love.

But life is rarely that simple. If yours is, then give thanks to God for such a gift, and do not treat your happy state as a platform from which to throw stones. Most marriages encounter problems. Not every one waits until marriage. An unknown proportion of people do not find sexual expression easy or possible, even within a committed relationship. Not all married couples are convinced that sex not open to conception is wrong or anything other than prudent. Some are not inclined to opposite-sex unions. And finally, almost the whole world population has or has had prolonged experience of non-relational sex, otherwise called masturbation, during either adolescence or periods of solitude or in a marriage which cannot satisfy their natural needs.

Are we to call all these people 'intrinsically disordered'? No, says the Church, and if anyone tells you that it does, they are telling you about their own hang-ups, or those of a section of the Church on earth, and not about the Church's magisterium instituted by Christ and guided by the Holy Spirit. In that case, are we to call the acts which such situations involve 'intrinsically disordered'?

Yes, but this is not actually a very big or alarming statement if it is understood properly. It means that these ways of behaving and living contradict the two principles mentioned above; in other words that they fall short of the image of God that we are called to be. If you look around the world, to be in such a state is not very surprising. Two points need to be borne in mind here with equal weight. The first is that the image of God is something we are called to, but over our whole lives. It is what we are growing towards, not what we are. To despair of our current position, whatever it may be, is therefore to lose the possibility of change in the future, of growing out of things we are now trapped in, but from which we want to be free.

The second point is to do with guilt. You may feel you are not trapped in a disordered situation, and that you have no desire to get out of it. An act may be intrinsically disordered. But this means that our actual guilt is relative to other factors, including the good old-fashioned ones of knowledge, freedom of choice and intention. Few couples use condoms as a deliberate rebellion against the divine order in creation; they do so because they cannot think of any alternative. Not many homosexuals see themselves as doing anything other than acting naturally. Two young people living together, unmarried, are not treating each other as sources of casual, irresponsible pleasure, and may not be particularly aware of the difference marriage can make. And maybe this is how the world is, made up of how we are. The Gospel is all about God's response to that state, not a command to somehow, straight away, achieve a perfection that may well seem arid and pointless. The Church is all about making God's forgiveness known, bringing people into contact with Jesus, in the faith that he comes to them where they are, and expects nobody to walk upon the water.

The Catholic Church is called to present to all ages a demanding understanding and ethic of marriage and sexuality, one that is often difficult to realize in practice but which all should continually strive to make their own. The Church is also aware that people may fail to live consistently what she teaches. Pastoral understanding is brought to bear on such failure; the Church does not reject such people, but wishes to walk with them in order to guide them to a fuller understanding and realization of the teaching she holds to be God-given.

Basil Hume, *Origins*, No. 45, p. 768

If you have heard anything different from that, you have not heard the Church, whoever it was who may have been speaking for her. The teaching is very clear and we know what it is. The application in the life of any particular soul is complex; it changes through life if we grow in knowledge of God, and is something always to be handled with sensitivity and the love of Christ. Here is one brief further example of the principles applied.

Artificial birth control

Perhaps, on the other hand, we try to obey the prohibition of artificial contraception. What tension does that cause in families? What kind of attitude to human sexuality? What havoc is wreaked in a child's life for how long by the dawning realization that he was an 'unwanted' child? How do we stop ourselves becoming the self-hating, repressed Catholics that are so useful to journalists?

It is almost impossible to talk sense on this issue and to be understood. The discussion can retreat into legalisms and technicalities. And all too often, whether one agrees with the Church or not, one has some kind of impression along the following lines, looking at the Pope, the bishops and the priests:

> But woe to you, scribes and Pharisees, because you shut the kingdom of heaven against people, for you neither enter yourselves, nor allow those who would enter to go in. You tithe mint and dill and cummin, and have neglected the weightier matters of the law; justice and mercy and faith.
>
> Matthew 23:13, 23

Contraception is such a difficult, involved and emotive subject, and so close to one of the most sensitive and personally important areas of human life. Contraception, the prevention of conception, is a very different matter from abortion, in which a human life is taken. Few Catholics have a problem with saying that abortion is wrong as a directly intended killing of a baby, whether or not he or she is yet old enough to be independently viable. But one should also be aware that such a teaching rules out some methods of contraception, including any which allow conception (the sperm fertilizing the ovum) but not implantation within the womb. Such methods include the coil and the morning-after pill. Intuitively, there is a moral difference between preventing an egg being fertilized and preventing a fertilized egg, already a human person, from being implanted.

There is not scope here to treat the issue of abortion as fully as it needs. It is a complicated issue and perhaps the first thing to say is that, for a woman or a couple facing a choice whether to have an abortion or to go ahead with the pregnancy, neither choice is easy. Indeed, to be facing the dilemma at all is one of the hardest situations we can encounter. The Church is undoubtedly correct in teaching that all human persons have a right to life. This is something that goes beyond issues of choice or culture. All human persons have a right to life. Things get complex when one asks what is a human person; to which the Church responds that every one of us is a human person from the moment of conception. Things get complex again when one asks what can be done in terms of politics. People argue that in a pluralist society one cannot impose this belief on others by law. On the other hand, if we believe something to be wrong, we might think it justified to stop people doing it; after all the same rationale is used to justify Western military intervention in support of human rights.

It is a deeply emotive issue. It is also an issue which needs to be considered from the point of view of those who face such a momentous choice. To end the life of a child is never something done lightly by people of good will or faith. The situation can be a severe tangle of conflicting desires and fears. It is understandable that a woman who has become pregnant after being raped may feel unable to carry a child with such associations. It is understandable that a young couple, for whom pregnancy is a nasty surprise for which they are not yet ready, should be filled with panic and a feeling that adult responsibility has hit them too fast. Just as easy to understand is the medical logic which dictates that if both mother and child in the womb are under threat of death, the mother's life must come first (though mothers themselves often differ on this. One lady I have talked with on this faced such a choice. The doctors said that if she died then both she and the baby would die, while if she lived she could still have another baby; to which she replied, 'Yes, but not this one.' Happily they both lived.)

Within each of these cases one might see a clear principle; a human life is at stake, whatever the causes and other issues. But people in those situations do not have the benefit of clarity. They need help, whatever they decide. They need help to try and see wood for trees, to sort out desires and fears, to step back from panic or resentment or fear. We can say easily that there is something very wrong with a culture in which thousands of abortions happen each day. And that is true. But many of those cases are not situations where people are acting freely, with the benefit of direct decision and no doubts. Our society urgently needs to hear alternative proposals to the culture of death. Such proposals must contain messages of hope to those in fear, and ways in which it can be easy for people to choose life, for unborn children and for themselves. There are, indeed, many initiatives and organizations that offer help (both moral and practical) to young mothers or people in dilemmas they cannot solve. A hand must be held out above all to men and women for whom the choice cannot be reversed, who have had, or decided with a partner to have, or persuaded someone to have an abortion. The harm which they have done to a human life is in some senses at least matched by the harm they have done to themselves. The Church always offers a way of healing. This is not a way of forgetfulness; things done cannot be undone, and some things we bear for life. But the Lamb of God who bears the sins of the world will have mercy on us if we ask him.

Contraception, while a smaller issue, has some of the same weight of dilemma and guilt for many. It is, however, a moral issue like any other. We listen to the Church, and do our best to understand and apply the teaching where and how we live. As with all matters of right and wrong, the final judgement is with your conscience. Using robust common sense is only rarely an objective moral wrong.

But we do need to look quite closely at what the Church really does teach, because there has been so much muddle and grief, not always helped by over-simplified presentation by clergy, either trying to soften or to underline a teaching which was never black and white in the first place.

The essence of the Church's teaching on contraception is set out in the encyclical letter of Pope Paul VI called *Humanae Vitae*. This was published in 1968 after a long process of discussion and consultation. The Pope set aside the recommendation of his commission and left the traditional teaching unchanged. This was a surprise and a shock to many people and has caused problems ever since. As a result, it is one of the most misunderstood documents in the history of the Church.

One of the reasons for this is that it is very tempting to skip through to 'the answer'. If you do that, then you get what you deserve:

> the direct interruption of the generative process already begun ... is excluded as lawful means of controlling the birth of children ... It is a serious error to think that a whole married life of otherwise normal relations can justify sexual intercourse which is deliberately contraceptive and so intrinsically wrong.
>
> *Humanae Vitae*, 14

This is a slap in the face. It is also understandably offensive to people who actually do live a whole and wholesome married life. All one can do is repeat a plea to read the teaching in context. On the other hand, if such a straight-down-the-line condemnation seems just the thing to you, I invite you to look with sympathy and understanding on those whose lives are not as simple as yours. Roughly half, the less-read half, of *Humanae Vitae* makes the same plea, if you will forgive the rather lofty and dated language.

> Husbands and wives should take up the burden appointed to them, willingly, in the spirit of faith and of that hope which 'does not disappoint us, because God's love has been poured into our hearts through the Holy Spirit who has been given to us' (Romans 5:5). Then let them beg the help of God with unremitting prayer and most of all let them drink deep of grace and charity from that unfailing fount which is the Eucharist.
>
> If, however, sin still exercises its hold over them, they are not to lose heart. Rather must they, humble and persevering, have recourse to the mercy of God, abundantly bestowed in the sacrament of penance. In this way, for sure, they will be able to reach the perfection of married life.
>
> *Humanae Vitae*, 25

So the choice is not necessarily between being a Catholic and using contraception, between going to Mass and communion and having a naturally expressed sexual love. If you have a chance to read through the whole encyclical, you may find your marriage strengthened and deepened by its vision.

But the document may retain for you a sense of detachment from the real world. Many couples will tell you that a whole and wholesome married life can be lived with contraception as part of responsible family planning, that it does not necessarily destroy the bond of love expressed sexually. In our time, being so used to technology and medicine on a large scale, we find it hard to understand the difference between so-called 'natural' methods and using a drug or a sheath. Here, as with every other moral issue, there is place for a responsible decision according to conscience. Hear the Church, understand its reasons, and then act with integrity. This is not watering down the papal teaching any more than saying you can kill in a just war or tell a white lie to avert major catastrophe. Yes, killing and lying are always wrong, but we do not always bear the guilt in a world which forces them upon us.

The Pope's point might be stretched to say that contraception is morally wrong; but it is only a sin, like any other sin. And as with any other issue, if we really cannot agree, try as we might, then we have at least tried, and Jesus Christ will not turn us away.

Chapter 21

SUICIDE

You shall not be put to shame or confounded to all eternity.

Isaiah 45:17

You may find that this chapter upsets you. It is a sad fact that almost everyone knows someone who has killed themselves. Maybe you can feel the roots of such an act in yourself. Suicide is a taboo subject; it rattles our bars too much.

Yet it has to be faced that more and more people are taking their own lives. We will look separately at the issue of euthanasia, when seriously ill people accelerate the process of dying in the hope of escaping pain (see chapter 23). Here, the concern is with people who find that normal life simply cannot go on.

Why is light given to one that is in misery,
and life to the bitter in soul,
who long for death, but it comes not,
and dig for it more than for hid treasures;
who rejoice and are glad,
when they find the grave?

Job 3:20–2

In the past, suicides were treated with some vindictiveness. Often denied a proper funeral, they could not be buried in consecrated ground. To attempt and fail was to face a life of stigma, and, in some countries, prosecution and even the death penalty. In moral terms, suicide was equated with the sin of despair – the denial of all hope, and the refusal to believe in the love of God. The phrase 'commit suicide' has all the resonance of a terrible crime: 'commit murder', 'commit treason'.

There is, of course, an association with Judas Iscariot, who, according to one tradition, hanged himself in remorse at having betrayed Jesus. The thought is almost that this is the only sufficiently depraved end for such a wicked man. Most people do have a conscious or unconscious association of suicide and the depression which precedes it as a sign of religious failure. One should surely gain hope from the good news, from the support of a Christian community. Pull yourself together, say your prayers, and all shall be well.

Everyone experiences shock and grief differently. But a common reaction to the suicide of a loved one is anger. How could he do this to us? What about the children? We gave her all she wanted; how can she have been so selfish? The assumption is that the suicidal are so bound up in their own misery that they care nothing for us any more. As a result, we fear introspection, disapprove of people who are wrapped up in themselves. A young man who may, after much hesitation, confess to a trusted friend that he is tempted to self-destruction, tends to be reminded of the blessings of his life, and the grief and havoc he would create in the lives of his loved ones. Sometimes, that is exactly the wrong thing to say.

One of the most chilling things about suicide is that it is contagious. Once the train of thought is started, even before it is acted upon, it can generate thoughts in the mind of another. The less we fear, though, the more we can help. In this chapter, I want to describe, so far as it can be described, what happens in the mind of someone who commits suicide. Maybe it will help you understand and give consolation to a depressed friend or relative. Maybe it will lighten some of the pain, if you have lost someone through suicide. Then we can set it in the light of the Good News of Jesus, who once said 'not one shall be lost'.

The clearest description of a suicidal mind that I have read is by Boris Pasternak in his 'Sketch for an Autobiography'. Here it is:

> A young man who decides to commit suicide puts a full stop to his being, he turns his back on his past, and declares himself bankrupt and his memories to be unreal. They can no longer help or save him; he has put himself beyond their reach.
>
> The continuity of his inner life is broken, and his personality is at an end. And perhaps what finally makes him kill himself is not the

firmness of his resolve but the unbearable quality of this anguish which belongs to no one, of this suffering in the absence of the sufferer, which is empty because his life has stopped and he can no longer feel it.

It is worth looking quite carefully at your reactions to this passage. If you think something like, 'Oh, what a lot of waffly nonsense,' then it is not an experience which you have shared. This makes it difficult to imagine, and perhaps you think it is not real. You may also share one or more of the following opinions:

- Suicide is only a problem for a few disturbed people.
- People who attempt suicide are only thinking of themselves.
- Depressed people should realize that we all have tough times, pull themselves together and get on with life.

These are taken from a Samaritans survey into suicide among young people, and are held by just over a third of people aged eighteen to twenty-four. At odds with this are the facts that:

- about a third of young people know someone who has died by suicide
- suicide is the second most common form of death (20 per cent) in that age group
- the rate of suicide in young men has doubled over the last decade.

The situation in the general population is not very dissimilar. The Samaritans, an organization devoted to listening to people in desperation, log one call every eight seconds.

Maybe this is a symptom of a society gone soft, where counsellors are drafted in on the smallest pretexts. Maybe much suicidal or depressive behaviour is attention seeking; for example, the hysterical girl who takes an 'overdose' and then rings the ambulance. But then, maybe, you will acknowledge that to say this is just to redefine the problem of why it happens.

To end one's own life is, after all, a last resort attempted against all the biological and psychological instincts for self-preservation. This is not a chapter for sceptics. If you are one of these, I just invite you to reflect how tough you really are.

But if you are one of the bewildered or fearful; if you do contemplate killing yourself, or have contemplated it, for whatever reason; if you love someone who has tried and failed; if you mourn someone who succeeded; if you are angry with them, or do not understand, then listen to this:

> *Blessed are the poor in spirit, for theirs is the Kingdom of Heaven.*
> *Blessed are those who weep now, for you shall be comforted.*
> *All that the Father gives me will come to me,*
> *and whoever comes to me,*
> *I shall not turn him away.*
> *My Father, who has given them to me,*
> *is greater than all,*
> *and no one is able to snatch them out of His hand.*

Why?

Why did she do it? What did I do wrong? Why didn't he listen to me? Why was she so selfish? Why didn't he come to me for help? Why can't I talk to people about it? Why can't I forgive him? Why did she forget our children? Why did he not know that we would still love him, no matter what? Why can't I follow her too?

These are questions without general answers. They are questions that mock anyone left behind by another's suicide. Perhaps it would help to enter a little into the suicidal mind.

Nobody really chooses to kill themselves. They die because it seems the only option, the only thing to do next. Almost universally, it is the only way to escape from overwhelming mental pain. Here is an account from a survivor, who jumped off a high balcony:

> I was so desperate. I felt, my God, I can't face this thing. Everything was like a terrible whirlpool of confusion. And I thought to myself, there's only one thing to do. I just have to lose consciousness. That's the only way to get away from it. And the only way to lose consciousness, I thought, was to jump off something good and high.
>
> And then I got to the fifth floor, and everything just got very dark all of a sudden, and all I could see was this balcony. Everything around it just blacked out. It was just like a circle. That was all I could see. Just the balcony. And I climbed over it and just let go. I was so desperate.

This is a very visual description of something common to nearly every suicide attempt. The field of thought shrinks, constricts. Pain narrows the mind to the single goal of escape. Friends, family, the bright side of life are not forgotten, but they do become invisible. No thought which conflicts with the overmastering need to 'get out' can enter the mind.

Past a certain point of closure, there seems little that anyone can do, except to remove or minimize physical opportunities. Sadly, it is possible for somebody to become 'closed' in this sense for some time before an attempt makes the constriction visible to others. Sometimes they give hints: occasional talk of death, making a new will for no apparent reason, even just tidying their room. But these are so much easier to see in hindsight. You may well have had no way of knowing.

The only way to get through the closed doors is to try to widen the options. A young woman who swallows painkillers because her boyfriend has left her, has lost sight of all the other men in the world. A man who jumps into a river on the way home from being sacked cannot see the loving wife and kids just further down the road. A young adolescent who hangs himself after a family row has blotted out the forgiving love of his parents.

Religion is not always a good option here. Suppose you tried this as advice:

> We are stewards, not owners of the life God has entrusted to us. It is not ours to dispose of.
>
> Suicide contradicts the natural inclination of the human being to preserve and perpetuate his life. It is gravely contrary to the just love of self. It likewise offends love of neighbour because it unjustly breaks the ties of solidarity with family, nation and other human societies to which we continue to have obligations. Suicide is contrary to love for the living God.
>
> *Catechism of the Catholic Church*, 2280–81

Of course, this is true, and it underlies much of the reaction of anger that one can have towards a suicide, and their apparent selfishness. The chances are, however, that someone on the edge already knows that. Emphasizing it may only increase their already bitter self-condemnation. For them, suicide is already inevitable, because it is the only resort left; they already feel damned, without adding our condemnation. 'Think of the children' will work only as a means of helping the person see that their closed world is not the real one, that although the job has been lost, there are still the children. It will be not be much use as an exhortation to for God's sake think of someone else for a change.

Suicide happens when mental anguish exceeds resources for dealing with pain. Everyone is different in what hurts and how much, and how much they can stand. We have to try either to reduce the pain, or help find or provide resources to deal with it. Much of what we might say could easily turn a possible resource into a burden.

But that need not be a source of guilt if you feel that you may have 'got it wrong'. The mind of a suicidal person is beyond even their own understanding. Maybe you cannot or could not help in any active way. You may wish you could, and if so, then you probably do or did all that could be done.

In fact, what a suicidal person needs from you is exactly the same attitude which you yourself might need in coping with another's death. Suppose we believe Jesus when he says that 'All whom the Father gives to me shall come to me.' Remember who is saying this:

> We do not have a high priest who is unable to sympathize with our weaknesses, but one who in every respect has been tempted as we are, yet without sin. Let us then with confidence draw near to the throne of grace, to receive mercy and find grace to help in time of need.
>
> Hebrews 4:15–16

If you want grace to help in someone's time of need, it will come to you, from Christ who on his cross exclaimed, 'My God, my God, why have you forsaken me?' If you cannot reconcile your questions in the aftermath of a suicide, draw near in confidence to Jesus who 'during his life on earth, offered up prayers and supplications, aloud and in silent tears, to him who was able to save him from death' (Hebrews 5:7). Christ himself has known the agony of that closure from the inside and from the outside, and you can be sure that he was in it and is in it with your loved one. 'Whoever comes to me, I shall not turn him away.'

Help me

Suicide involves a cruel paradox, for it is almost invariably the case that someone who kills themselves does not want to die. At one extreme is the phenomenon called 'para-suicide' where death is never intended, although these 'attempts' can be tragically successful. A typical example is the slashing of wrists and arms, where the aim seems to be to express violence against the self, and a dramatic, if unconscious, plea for help.

But a full-scale suicide is most deeply tragic in that to the last moment the poor man or woman or child is desperate for another option to present itself. The woman already mentioned describes how she walked dressed only in a hospital gown on a narrow steel beam, high above the ground, 'hoping that someone would see me out of all those windows; the whole building is made of glass'.

If you feel you have to take your life, what is Jesus saying to you? Maybe you are hearing something like this:

> 'By despair, you cease to hope for your personal salvation from God, for help in attaining it or for the forgiveness of your sins. Despair is contrary to My goodness and to My justice and to My mercy; for I am always faithful to my promises.'
>
> cf. *Catechism of the Catholic Church*, 2091

Once again, this is very good theology, and it is true. But it is a definition of what you suffer, not the way to another option. How about this instead?

> Blessed are the poor in spirit, for yours is the Kingdom of Heaven.
> Blessed are you who weep now, for you shall be comforted.

Jesus does not condemn you, he blesses you. Now, at the worst moment of your life, he blesses you. No consolation, no magic, no solution; not now, anyway. Just blessing. Not to make you feel worse; you probably can't feel any worse. With your despair there is another fact, just as stark: the blessing of God upon you now and always, whatever you do next.

> The light shines in the darkness, and the darkness has not overcome it.
>
> John 1:5

Since there is light, and there is blessing, then death is not the last word. This means that there is more than death present now. Maybe you can listen to that blessing, and speak to him who is blessing.

If Jesus can bless and listen, perhaps someone else can as well. You know that there are people who will simply give you time, without judgement and advice. That is another option.

Chapter 22

BLUE PIGS

You can turn man back into dust.

Psalm 90:3

The suicide issue has become more pressing as the pace of life quickens and people can feel left behind. We think more and more that what is 'normal' and acceptable as success, consists in having lots of things. Among those things are, as well as a car and a mobile phone, being 'happy' and in control of one's own life. But such a sense is threatened by something out of our control, though we have made it. This is the potential of science and industrial (or even post-industrial) culture to wreck the place where we live. There is even the possibility of changing who and what human beings are. It is not easy to be rational about such a threat; in the UK, there is near-hysteria at the thought of genetically modified corn getting into the food chain. But just as irrational is to suppose, as we supposed for a couple of centuries before Hiroshima, that the advance of scientific knowledge is inevitably and always a good thing that cannot go wrong.

The Church has sometimes seemed to be a bit at a loss when it comes to science and scientific research. I have already mentioned the Galileo debacle, from which we have still not quite recovered. Scientists can easily resent Christians asking ethical questions, and see it as old-fashioned obscurantism, a simple fear of progress and the way it might inevitably erode our beliefs as science and its world-view triumphs. Christians, in turn, may feel intimidated by the vast array of research projects in progress, each of them largely incomprehensible to all except specialists. Science carries with itself a myth of competence and omnipotence.

One should say in passing that there is absolutely no need for a believer to be afraid of science. Truth cannot contradict truth. It may not always be obvious how to fit the findings of science about the world into traditional faith, but this does not mean that they are incompatible, just that we need to work out what is what and how to reconcile apparent conflicts. This can even be good. For example, the fairly well established fact that the world and all in it was not made in seven (six, for pedants) days a few thousand years ago, has forced us into a much deeper understanding of God being present to the world at all times, rather than just starting it all off. Similarly, that we may have evolved in many stages from much simpler organisms makes the world a more, not a less, wonderful place. It also forces us to take God's action in creation as real and material, rather than just waving a spiritual wand at us. In this chapter we shall look at just one area, that of genetic research and its capabilities, simply to suggest that very easily grasped principles can help us work out what is right and what is wrong; even a scientist with little training in theology would manage!

Genetic engineering currently carries with it a particularly powerful air of omnipotence. It is talked about in wild language. The appearance a few years ago of Dolly the cloned sheep set people looking at friends and relations in a new light. We are told that a cloned human being is only a year away, so start planning now. It is not surprising that media presentation of the issues has rarely risen above such silly jokes. For genetic engineering (also called genetic manipulation, or, for real cognoscenti, recombinant DNA technology) is very clever and very complex. It lies beyond the understanding of all but a few highly trained individuals. Many of us are now accustomed to computer technology even if the physics and mathematics behind it remains mercifully obscure. Genetic engineering is not so domesticated, and never will be. The food consumer is becoming cynical about statements that 'there is no evidence of any risk ...' We are disinclined to become such evidence ourselves, but on the other hand, there is nothing else to eat. Good news tastes better than bad, and is swallowed so much more easily.

In the same way, most people are confused about genetic engineering. It sounds so good, that it might be too good. We have the technology; what are we to do with it? What benefits are held out? The sky is the limit. Genes are, after all, something to do with the basic code of life. You have your mother's eyes, your father's ears, and your own way of doing things. Jessica Rabbit, Roger's girl-friend in the hit cartoon film, says at one point: 'I can't help being bad. I'm just drawn that way.' It is easy to find sensational stories. Identical twins, separated ever since birth, have been known to come to a researcher's interview where they meet for the first time wearing identical shirts. Coincidence? Probably, except that their own children had first names in common. Genes are power, of life and death.

What can we do?

Maybe that is going too far. But it is impossible not to go too far. Disregarding the popular desire to engineer a consistently success-ful football team, the positive results already achieved are immense, and more widespread than you might think. Pharmacotherapy is being revolutionized, to the extent that anything written about what can be done is out of date the next day. For some years, micro-organisms have been used to produce antibiotics. But now, we can 'program' the bugs to produce other useful chemicals. Inserting mammalian genes into bacteria can cause them to pro-duce insulin, so vital for diabetics, growth hormones, and blood-clotting proteins needed by haemophiliacs. Research using the same techniques has produced a hitherto impossible hepatitis B vaccine, and is finding many clues to vaccines for malaria and AIDS. The point is that the micro-organisms can produce drugs and so on at a rate and cost that makes them realistically available to many more people.

In agriculture, there has been much noise recently about genet-ically modified food, that is, food made of corn or other crops that are new strains produced directly by genetic manipulation. Instead of the small taste-free tomatoes which grace British supermarkets, American citizens have access to genetically produced large taste-free tomatoes. If the company producing them reads that, I will be sued. Why? Because genetically modified organisms (GMOs) are big business; the right patent is a licence to print money. The US market for enzymes, essential catalysts for most of the processes within living things, was estimated as long ago as 1985 at $500 mil-lion. We can make plants that are tolerant of herbicides, which means you can blitz the field with chemicals that kill anything else. To deal with insects and other pests, we can make the plants indigestible to them. Or, going one better, we can make plants that grow their own insecticide, *Bacillus thuringensis*. The necessary gene has been successfully put into corn, cotton, soya beans, tobacco (maybe not so good) and, of course, tomatoes.

The benefits go far beyond more, cheaper or better-looking food. Agricultural products are of use in industry and elsewhere. For about $1 million you can make a flock of sheep genetically altered to produce the protein alpha-1 antitrypsin in their milk, to treat emphysema. Amgen, a Canadian company, can now design and make chickens that will lay eggs containing otherwise expensive drugs instead of the usual proteins. And silkworm caterpillars can be made that produce human insulin. Against this, producing cattle breeds that grow faster and produce more milk, or more woolly sheep, seems child's play

Hold on a minute! Surely our delight at the new world being made around us should be tempered with apprehension. Leaving aside scientific risks of the world being taken over by giant taste-free tomatoes after humans have succumbed to the unforeseen consequences of eating insecticide-bearing soya beans, there are other issues at stake. In particular, a Christian might pause at the repeated use of the phrase 'we can make'. Are we inviting our own nemesis, as we try to play God, to eat once more of the forbidden tree? Here, the ground becomes uneven, and the way ahead very hard to see. We can be cushioned by imaginary absurdities for a while, but the power now in our hands forces some very uncomfortable questions about who and what we are. The Italian psychologist Luigi Zoja has identified a discomfort at the heart of Western technological civilization:

> Progress today is so swift that we constantly exploit its recent innovations without having been able to establish any profound connection with the culture from which it derives ... Technological civilization forswears the celebration of its triumph not only because of its loss of access to the elevated planes of mythic language, but also because it harbours doubts and feelings of guilt about the meaning of its achievements. The achievements of western mankind are ever less experienced as a victory over the men of other civilizations; they seem instead to represent the general defeat of men by things.
>
> *Growth and Guilt*, p. 5

There are two distinct points here. First is the rate of growth of scientific possibilities. This has to some extent outstripped our ability to describe, interpret and evaluate. For example, is it correct to say, as the law does at present, that Kathy and Bill have parental rights over Sam, despite the fact that Sam grew from donated sperm and a donated ovum in a surrogate womb? We have little in the way of concepts and vocabulary that can decide this issue on the level of ethics. But it is real; it certainly matters to all the people involved.

We are in important senses not yet old enough to play with our toys. Yet there they are. These techniques and their possible extensions go far beyond what is 'natural'. Or do they? What is natural? Here, the first point merges with the second. Do we have the right to do these things? The Catholic Church is quite clear on *in vitro* fertilization: we don't. But that is a minority view. What is so unnatural that we cannot do it? Is not paracetamol unnatural in some sense? Invasive operations such as tonsillectomies are strange, violent actions, from one point of view. How can we find a difference between drinking tea and manufacturing whole new species; or how do we find that there is no difference?

Genetically modified organisms have entered the field of public ethics because it is now suggested that we should eat them. This causes an understandable, and justified, degree of apprehension. Hopefully, an understanding of the processes involved would lighten this a little. But it might leave the impression that we are dealing with technology so sophisticated that it is beyond anyone to say with assurance what consequences will result from its use. It might seem that there are too many 'dunno' statements in the governmental and corporate assurances. The public well remembers how safe thalidomide was thought to be, and how safe it actually was.

Genetic engineering, however, is on a larger scale by far. It is held out as the solution to third world starvation, as high-yielding crops that grow in the most surprising places can be produced and propagated. Medicines and vaccines can banish intractable illnesses into the land of memory, where they will join smallpox and others. Or does this hide for us those deep and nasty questions about life and death? Why do we want so much to banish disease? Why resort to technology when we can already produce enough food for everyone, but do not distribute it? Does not biotechnology simply continue the trend of reducing the earth's diversity into a few useful plant species? How much risk should we accept in the eternal quest for tomatoes with taste?

If the distinction made earlier is accepted, then one may say that we are simply not able to answer these questions. It has all happened so fast that it will be some time before we have grown alongside our possibilities. This has happened before. We have now the irony of the inhabitants of Europe, who have destroyed most of their natural forest, attempting to stop those of South America from destroying theirs. The discovery that commercial exploitation will eventually result in not enough for anyone has begun to take hold. But there is a long way to go.

Where to stop

Exactly the same can be said with regard to the issue of safety. This is why the BSE issue in United Kingdom agriculture has been such a muddle. We now spend a fortune trying to reduce to zero a risk smaller than those we blithely ignore, such as crossing the road. Sympathy for those who suffer after contracting a disease from eating BSE-infected beef quite rightly drives an attempt to understand and eradicate the condition, but our culture makes the question of relative value undecidable. We might say that no food, GMO or otherwise, should be on the shelf unless it is one hundred per cent safe. But we would get very thin.

If you have a happy attitude to technology, then you emphasize the advantages. There are bound to be risks: in fact, everything is risky, and all the prudent person can do is to minimize the chances of things going wrong. We have been doing that since the discovery of fire. Setbacks are not the fault of science and scientists per se. If a problem arises unforeseen, then one can say that most human endeavours, notably the discovery of fire, have involved problems to be solved. If the problem is deliberately caused, then it is often the result of individuals or groups acting unethically, as did, for example, some researchers in the Third Reich. We can, and need to, evolve and update ways to control the use of dangerous knowledge.

Clearly, if I use an axe to murder you instead of cutting wood for a fire to keep you alive, then it is wrong to blame the use of metal technology in arboriculture. But if your attitude to technology is less relaxed, then the fears and dangers are more apparent. Such is naturally the province of ecologists whose science largely consists in quantifying the deleterious results of misuse or use of other scientific disciplines. Either side is, at present, too strident, whether they talk of the miracles to come, or the horrors that await us. Maybe the situation is not so clear cut either way.

The matter comes to a head over the question of what is 'natural'. A genetic engineer might claim that all he or she is doing is accelerating a natural process. Humans have been practising a crude form of genetic engineering since the first dogs were domesticated around 10,000 BC. We have developed strains of cattle, sheep, wheat, and even of each other as we have assessed possible mates. It can take several years to develop a new crop strain by sexual reproduction. Genetic engineering merely bypasses the intermediate stages. As such, it is no different, and no more or less dangerous, than what we have done or misdone for years. To cry 'stop' is simply to refuse to progress further along an obvious line of development.

Such a view is widespread and disingenuous. By and large, the interesting GMOs come from putting the genes of one species into another. We put human genes into pigs, and bacterial genes into plants. This cannot happen in nature. Sexual reproduction cannot occur between distinct species (since that is the definition of a species), and so the required DNA complexes are not natural. Genetic change has come about by human selection and breeding, but it has taken centuries within which the plant or animal adapts to the environment and vice versa. We have also done it only with easy and obvious organisms, which means very few. But as Reiss and Straughan comment:

> Genetic engineering is far more ambitious. It seeks to change not only the species that provide us with food and drink, but also those involved in sewage disposal, pollution control and drug production. It also seeks to create microorganisms, plants and animals that can make human products, such as insulin, and even, possibly, to change the genetic make-up of humans.
>
> *Improving Nature?*, p. 5

Once one talks about manipulating human genes, the problems become yet more complex and more emotive. We have to start talking about genetic counselling and therapeutic abortions. Most people accept quite a high degree of exploitation of animals and plants, much of it far from benign. But manipulating human beings seems to be going a whole lot further, since it actually affects us, and not just a bunch of pigs or tomatoes. However, in the face of so much that is unknown or beyond one's own understanding, Catholics need not feel at a loss. What has been said so far is based simply on the ethics of prudence balancing what is useful. But we have other principles to apply and do so in many areas of research. For example, I said above that the Church has a clear position on *in vitro* fertilization. This is because the technique involves the creation of many 'spare' embryos who are frozen or killed after the successful implantation of the lucky winner.

When it comes to any form of scientific research or medical technique, anything which involves saying a human person is not a human person, or which denies their dignity or choice, can confidently be said to be wrong, for whatever reason it is done, and no matter how small or defenceless the person in question. The products and results of such research or manufacturing processes are tainted with the evil they involve. It is not going too far to speak of evil here; after all, what is happening is that our good instincts for survival become twisted towards surviving at any cost, to ourselves and to others. Similarly, it is clearly wrong to give people food that is not safe for the sake of making a profit. One must not be blinded by the technicalities of scientific research into thinking that the ethics lie beyond the common-sense everyday principles of justice and of love.

Chapter 23

ON THE SHELF

I will release you from slavery.

Exodus 5:6

It is a good life, if you do not weaken. Our culture is built on the assumption that things go well. This can be good. Optimism about what might happen is a necessary part of getting out of bed in the morning. Our liberation from fear that the sky will fall on our heads, or that a vengeful witch is going to curse the kettle so that it will never boil, is, on the whole, a gain.

Except that it leaves us rather poorly equipped to deal with life. Those who happily relegate religion to the superstition department have a point. Religion can very easily involve superstition, and usually does, even if the jinxes and good-luck charms we use in the developed world are more sophisticated and tasteful. The same is true of everyday life. Few people believe that walking under a ladder will bring bad luck, but few people walk under ladders. Few people think that prayers are magical spells, but most of us are aggrieved if they do not work.

Superstition, however, has two important ingredients. One is fear, and the other is taboo: things which are forbidden or not to be mentioned. In this sense, our modern culture is deeply superstitious. For all our liberation from belief in hobgoblins and witches, we are in some ways more frightened than our ancestors by things which they took as a normal part of life. For all our defences against cold, disease and hunger, we are far more vulnerable to vulnerability itself.

Suppose, for example, you are diagnosed with a terrible life-threatening illness. The assumption is that it can be treated and held off, if not cured. If it can't be, then often nobody seems quite sure what to say or do. The possibility that nothing can be done, and nothing said, is becoming too appalling. You can meet families in hospitals or hospices determined to avoid the thought of death. They talk briskly about medication, ask 'Are you comfortable?', bring flowers and fruit, do anything except face reality.

Our cultural need that everything should be OK and that nothing should go wrong – that, for example, we should be able to fight wars by bombing with no loss of life, at least on our side – has two disadvantages. First, it makes it much harder to cope when things do inevitably go wrong. Euphemisms such as 'collateral damage' or the quick, clean disposal of bodies in crematoria do, for some, make things easier. But in many situations in life, we actually need the pain in order to survive the experience, be it grief, post-natal depression or failing an examination. Truth is hard, but it does set free. Otherwise, one is like a man who will not stir from his chair and use crutches because he does not want to admit that his leg is broken.

The other side of this is an unfeeling bluntness that treats pain and anguish as part of life, something to be faced and got over: 'It's for your own good.' That is not true, either. It is a denial of someone else's pain so that I do not have to face it. If that sounds too abstract, then it is an experience known by almost all who mourn. It is also sometimes the reason why we consign elderly relatives to old people's homes (which now have a range of far more comfortable descriptions). Certainly, they can be cared for better by specialists than by me; certainly, it would be an awful, and perhaps impossible, distortion of my family life to include caring for them in it. I am not saying old folks' homes are wrong; it is just that we should be aware that, for some people if not for us, they fulfil the function of hiding from us the unwelcome decline of a deeply loved parent. In addition, old people can find themselves trapped in a cycle of anxiety and demand that becomes a vindictive or possessive selfishness. As such, they drive away relatives who cannot cope. Our culture makes it hard for us to accept our own decline as well as that of others. There are many other examples. In none of them are we culpable. But we should recognize the evasions in which we collude.

The second disadvantage is that we have to write off most of life. If you do not look like the girl in the advert, if your holiday is not as fun-filled as the brochure implied, if you lose from illness or simple discouragement the ability to live life as we are told it should be lived – pubbing, clubbing, fun with other beautiful people – then you are somehow suspect, defective. There is very little role in modern life for the elderly, disabled, long-term sick or unemployed. The ways of trying to cater for them, walkways, financial aid, etc., are becoming better understood and provided, but largely as a way of stopping them being a bother on our way to the shops. If you find that too much, then you have never walked past anyone begging in the street without at least a smile.

It is we who are strong who lose out, though. For our strength is illusory. It can be laid low by redundancy, by buying the wrong house, by the death of your spouse or child, or even by a tiny virus. It is a damaging illusion, because it cuts us off from other people by preventing us from sharing their frailty and them from seeing ours. Of course there are practicalities here. Nobody gets on in life by blubbering after a bad meeting or refusing to take decisions. But everybody benefits from mutual dependence, from the solidarity in fear and love that can cross generations, eliminate the difference between rich and poor, male and female. And if everybody benefits, you benefit too, 'in as much as every person needs others and draws enrichment from the gifts and charisms of all' (John Paul II, *Letter to the Elderly*, 10).

Living to the full

It might seem perverse to begin a section with this title by talking about death. The fact of death contradicts so much of what we want to believe, and most of what we live by. Few people have the courage to face death each moment of their lives. Nor is it entirely sensible to do so. Life would come to a stop; there would be no mortgages, no savings plans, and very little point in buying food for lunch tomorrow when you may well not be there.

But this is facetious. What we do not want to remember is that the sands are running out, and that nothing can stop them. Most of us can remember the awful moment at which death first became a reality, when our childhood world was fractured by a realization of impermanence. Most of us spend the rest of our lives fleeing from that reality. As a result, we can lose the point of life, since we so dread its end. Death contradicts our deepest instincts, outrages our sense of how things should be. Of all things most natural, it cannot be understood naturally; we can never quite take it in as fact or as possibility. In her splendid book, *When Parents Die*, Rebecca Abrams makes the following point:

> When a parent dies very unexpectedly, the shock is enormous. Your trust in the world is violated; the foundations of your life are shattered. A sudden death destroys your confidence that life is as you imagine it ... You expect life to be as you see it. Likewise you expect your parents to be alive.
>
> *When Parents Die*, p. 43

In other words, there is rebellion: this cannot be happening, it cannot be true. That revolt, the refusal to accept death, is not simply wishful thinking. It is pure outrage, the wrath, indeed, of God at the dissolution of life. Our instinct that life has to have a meaning is the deepest fact of our nature. It is our sense of the transcendent, of eternity. It is a sad fact of our fallen nature that this sense is awakened only by its denial in crisis and lifelessness. Just as youth is wasted on the young, so life is often wasted on the living. Yet it is available to us in large parts of the population, if only we look for it.

The encounter with death is what makes us alive, because it puts the whole of life into its due perspective. On the simplest level, if you thought this moment to be your last, you would live it to the full. If we really believed our lives to be surrounded by eternity, circumscribed by death, then we would really live each day to its full value, and to our own full value. Mortality does not contradict human dignity; it shows that we see only the beginnings.

Such an encounter is possible whenever we face our frailty and accept it as a part of who we are. The best way to do that is to face the vulnerability of another, and bring them peace. The story is told of St Hugh, bishop of Lincoln in the twelfth century, visiting a leper sanctuary. One of his clergy teased him by saying that if he was really holy he could cleanse the lepers by touching them. Hugh's response reveals not just his sanctity but a fundamental fact of the Gospel and of human life: 'It is their touch that makes me clean.'

Such cleansing lies in the power of all the people that our society can tend to write off: retired, unemployed, sick, and disabled, to name just a few. Those who are, for whatever reason, too weak to do anything, witness to the most important fact in creation, that

God created each person out of delight in him or herself, not in what they might do or build. We know that this is true because the definitive revelation of God in our world took the form of the extreme failure, indignity and uselessness of the Cross. The resurrection of Jesus is simply the consequence of the fact that God refuses to see any of his beloved human beings as futile or without any point.

It is for such reasons that the Catholic Church resists calls to legalize euthanasia. By this word, which means 'a good death', is meant the ending of a human life in the face of intolerable suffering. Usually this refers to someone who is enduring a terminal illness; it is almost a way of shortcutting the long and painful end that will come anyway. But it is an understandable temptation for any older person who feels that his or her own life has already run its useful course. Maybe they fear being a burden on their family. Perhaps the thought of gradual decay of body or mind is too terrifying to confront. As I say, a desire for euthanasia prompted by such considerations is understandable; it is quite normal and usually not at all sinful for, say, a cancer sufferer to actively wish to die. The problem is in saying that a human being at any stage, under any disability, is sufficiently worthless to be simply switched off. The fault lies in a culture which persuades us that pain is unbearable and that to support someone is a burden. That is not to say that a suffering family should see sense in the pain or decline of a loved and respected parent or friend. It is to say that God is with them, and that God's presence is always active love. Our task is to help people bear what life brings, not pretend that all is well, at the cost of the life of a child of God. But we must be always considerate of the strain that people find themselves under.

Of course, there are more subtle ways of denying human value, often too subtle for us to notice or admit. The elderly are safely confined in homes, the mentally ill consigned to the care of professionals. Perhaps the most widespread example of the tendency is what happens to people when they retire. This can be a very traumatic time both for the person retiring and for their family and friends. A man or woman who stops work can very easily feel useless. Unfortunately the leisure image of retirement does not help this at all: pictures of happy septuagenarians playing golf or going on cruises. The welcome thoughts that now I can put my feet up and relax, enjoy some of the gains of my working life, spend time at home with my husband or wife, take the grandchildren out, devote time to neglected hobbies, are genuine. But they can hide an equally genuine, though less welcome, feeling of 'Is that it, then?' The person who can suddenly give up a job and retain a sense of value without any sneaking anxiety is rare indeed.

The impact can be deeper and more wide-ranging than just feeling down, however. It is very frequent for marriages to go through prolonged difficulties following the retirement of one or both partners. Not only does the retired person feel a bit at a loose end, but the couple are seeing more of each other than they have since, perhaps, their courting days, or even more. In the intervening time, they have changed, and there is much to learn about each other. Human beings do not learn best in pressured environments from which they cannot escape, and so there can build up all kinds of frustrations and resentments that neither wife nor husband understand and think are entirely their own fault or that of the other. Almost anything can go wrong with a marriage at this stage, and it requires immense patience and a sense of one's true worth. You may indeed be a useless and clumsy clot about the house, you may no longer be the man she married (or vice versa). But you have a lot to give, even in the experience of difficulty:

> How many people find understanding and comfort from elderly people who may be lonely or ill and yet are able to instil courage by their loving advice, their silent prayers, or their witness of suffering borne with patient acceptance.
>
> John Paul II, *Letter to the Elderly*, 12

That is something all the busy and useful people very much need to find, and which a fast-moving world needs to have at its centre. The same applies to everyone who feels they no longer have anything to give. You have in truth the most vital ministry of all, sharing with the Lamb of God in bearing the sins of his people. God chooses the weak and makes them strong in bearing witness to him. This is why we honour martyrs; people put to death for their faith show not just strength of faith, but their helplessness in the face of the world's malice. Even in happier times, when we are not necessarily executed, precisely because the world thinks we are of no account, we expose the narrowness of its values, and the deeper truth of God's love for it.

No amount of thinking like that will take away pain and suffering. But it will unite it with that of the Lord. If nobody will stand with you, then you can stand with him at the foot of the Cross. If you are rejected, then you can accept him who is rejected with you.

AFTERWORD

Being Catholic Today

Know that I am with you always.

Matthew 28:20

I remember as a small child visiting the Holy Sepulchre, the place where, according to tradition, Jesus' body was laid after the crucifixion. Two things stood out and remained in my mind. The first was the number of people. There is only really room for one or two people at a time in the Sepulchre, and the entrance is quite narrow. So if there is a queue, it can take some time to get in, and you may not get much time in there. Lots of people, eager to see the tomb from which our Saviour rose to conquer death, each person having to wait patiently. The second impression was a matter for disappointment. I expected a holy place, at least some kind of echo of the event that had happened there when the universe changed for ever. As we put it in the Eastertide prayer:

In him a new age has dawned,
The long reign of sin is ended,
A broken world has been renewed
And we are once again made whole.

Roman Missal, Preface of Easter IV

But there was no echo. In fact, there was nothing at all; just a stone shelf and my own questions about why the place was empty of 'vibes'. It was not until I was lucky enough to go again, and had the same experience (without the crowds, though, because I went very early in the morning), that I made a connection with the words of the angel to the women looking for Christ's body on Easter morning. They are words for you too, spoken from God, wherever you find yourself. Listen to them in your heart:

> There is no need for you to be afraid. I know you are looking for Jesus. He is not here, for he has risen.
>
> Matthew 28:5

Whom do you seek today? There is in each of us a sense of need, a sense of something to be looked for. Of course, most of us disguise it, cover it up with achievements or mundane worries. Only one thing can give us true peace, lead us where we really want to go, and that is to walk with Jesus.

It can be, and most of the time is, hard to find him. Life can be rather like the queue to see the tomb, and in our anxiety and frustration to be fulfilled and safe we trample each other like commuters on the London Underground or the New York subway. The irony is that whatever we try and grab, Jesus is not there, not even in the empty tomb where many of us are forced to dwell.

It is only hard to find Christ if we forget that he is already with us, holding out his hands to take ours and fill them with all we could ever want or need. Let us think for a moment how to recognize him. What were the signs of the resurrection as told in the Gospels?

> In the evening of that same day, the first day of the week, the doors were closed in the room where the disciples were, for fear of the Jews. Jesus came and stood among them. He said to them, 'Peace be with you', and showed them his hands and his side.
>
> John 20:19–20

The disciples were not filled with joy, not full of confident faith, not ready to take on the whole world and triumph. They skulked and hid, knowing their weakness and not daring to move. So Jesus, as well as offering peace, showed them his hands and side. The signs Christ chose to show his risen presence to the disciples were his wounds.

It is the same for us. To find the Lord, look at what you lack, look at what you fear, look at what fates you strive to avoid. That is where Jesus is at work, if only you let him. That is where you can work for him. Because you know in yourself your need of him, you can serve that same need in other people, simply by treating them like human beings. These are the two commandments on which all is based: to love the Lord God with *all* your being, and to love your neighbour as yourself.

Being Catholic comes down to that. We face so many problems (or 'challenges', if you like management-speak). In many ways the Church seems doomed: falling Mass attendance, two lost generations, failing to listen, out of touch. Many of its wounds are all the worse for being self-inflicted.

So, is there a future? There is indeed. Soon after his appointment as Archbishop of Westminster, Cormac Murphy O'Connor said in an interview: 'We are not asked to be successful. We are asked to be faithful.' To be faithful is to realize that in each problem, in each wound, Jesus is present to heal and to bless. It is the faults and shortcomings of human beings that interest him, it is there that he works; for he came to call not the righteous, but sinners to repentance.

The challenge of being Catholic today is to be faithful to that vision, and to be faithful to each other in sharing our faults in the forgiveness of Christ. I hope you have enjoyed our conversation. Maybe you have found some helpful things. You have most likely found things to disagree with too. If the family can talk, the family can face a future together, united and respecting the fact that we are different people. The Church is not 'the Church', it is you and me, standing before the Father. If we stand together in love and forgiveness, then Jesus stands with us too.

There is a custom among monks of ending letters with a particular phrase, and I leave that as our final thought. *Oremus pro invicem*; let us pray for each other.